Multicultural Customer Service

Providing Outstanding Service Across Cultures

Multicultural Customer Service

Providing Outstanding Service Across Cultures

LESLIE AGUILAR
LINDA STOKES

Business Skills Express Series

IRWIN
Professional Publishing

MIRROR PRESS®

Irwin Professional Book Team

Mirror Press:	David R. Helmstadter
	Carla F. Tishler

Marketing manager:	Carl Helwing
Project editor:	Amy E. Lund
Production supervisor:	Pat Frederickson
Designer:	Larry Cope
Compositor:	Alexander Graphics, Ltd.
Typeface:	12/14 Criterion
Printer:	Malloy Lithographing, Inc.

**Times Mirror
Higher Education Group**

Library of Congress Cataloging-in-Publication Data

Aguilar, Leslie
    Multicultural customer service : providing outstanding service
across cultures / Leslie Aguilar, Linda Stokes.
       p.   cm.—(Business skills express series)
    Includes index.
    ISBN 0-7863-0332-8
    1. Customer services—Social aspects. 2. Intercultural
communication.   I. Stokes, Linda, 1954– . II. Title.
III. Series.
HF5415.5.A37   1996
658.8'12—dc20   95–33465

PREFACE

Globalization, technology, and availability of transportation make it easier and more convenient than ever before for people to take advantage of the many tourist destinations, services, and opportunities to visit friends and family around the world. At the same time, business travel has expanded as organizations compete on a global scale.

Providing quality customer service to these travelers and visitors is an important aspect of today's business strategy and of your jobs as service providers. Meeting the needs of all the customers who walk through your doors with their various expectations and needs requires additional knowledge and skills. By working with customers in a way that values them as individuals, you can satisfy them and keep them returning.

Because of the ease and increased frequency of travel, the customer who walks through your door, calls on the phone, wishes to purchase your product or service, or simply asks a question, may look, act, think, and have very different ideas about customer service than the customer who you have traditionally served. A changing customer base creates special challenges and opportunities for organizations and for service providers who are committed to finding ways to provide customer service that meets individual needs.

This book will help you enhance the knowledge and skills that you already have so that you can provide exceptional service to all of your customers—the ones who speak your language and share similar customs and dress—and those who don't. The desire for applying your learning and for serving all customers in an outstanding way comes from within.

We begin this book by looking at customer service in general and then more specifically at multicultural customer service. Then, you will enhance your understanding of culture in order to better serve customers from around the world and multicultural customers from within your own community. You will explore needs specific to multicultural customers and gain tips for communicating across cultures and languages. Lastly, you will read about some of the outstanding multicultural service examples that we have found in various industries across the United States.

We hope that you enjoy reading our book and participating in the exercises, and that you gain new insights and skills as a result. As you read the scenarios and examples that represent a variety of industries and service providers, please take time to personalize the concepts for yourself by applying them to your job.

Because we, like you, are continuously learning, we invite you to contact us with examples, stories, or questions concerning multicultural customer service. You may call us at our offices at:

Leslie Aguilar
International Training and
    Development
407-859-1191

Linda Stokes
Prism International
407-860-5040

ABOUT THE AUTHORS

Leslie Aguilar is president of International Training and Development. The firm helps individuals and organizations succeed in an increasingly diverse and global marketplace. Programs include diversity, multicultural customer service, international transitions, and cross-cultural communication.

Previously, Leslie was on the staff of The Walt Disney Company for 15 years. She began her Disney career in customer service, where she assisted visitors from around the world. After leaving Central Florida to live in Mexico, Spain, France, and Switzerland, and to complete studies in foreign language, she spent several years as assistant director of an international hospitality school. Leslie later returned to the Disney professional staff where she developed and presented training programs, primarily in the area of cultural awareness and transition for American and European expatriate staff. Leslie is an ESOL (English for Speakers of Other Languages) instructor. She is committed to creating a community where individuals work together and serve each other effectively and respectfully across language, ethnic and racial, cultural, gender, age, abilities, lifestyle, and individual differences.

Linda Stokes is the president of Prism International, Inc., a diversity training and consulting company located in Florida. Prism's trainers and consultants assist individuals, work teams, and organizations with diversity and the inclusion of all available human resources to meet organizational, employee, and customer needs. Linda has consulted and trained in the areas of customer service and diversity in over 100 organizations throughout the United States, Canada, and the U.K. Her corporate experience spans many industries: finance, government, utilities, airlines, healthcare, hotels, theme parks, and telecommunications. Along with her corporate responsibilities, she also volunteers time to local schools where she presents diversity programs to second and third graders.

ABOUT IRWIN PROFESSIONAL PUBLISHING

Irwin Professional Publishing is the nation's premier publisher of business books. As a Times Mirror company, we work closely with Times Mirror training organizations, including Zenger-Miller, Inc.; Learning International, Inc.; and Kaset International to serve the training needs of business and industry.

About the Business Skills Express Series

This expanding series of authoritative, concise, and fast-paced books delivers high-quality training on key business topics at a remarkably affordable cost. The series will help managers, supervisors, and frontline personnel in organizations of all sizes and types hone their business skills while enhancing job performance and career satisfaction.

Business Skills Express books are ideal for employee seminars, independent self-study, on-the-job training, and classroom-based instruction. Express books are also convenient-to-use references at work.

ACKNOWLEDGEMENTS

Over 30 organizations and individuals shared their time and talent with us in the creation of this book. While all their names do not appear in the text, their experiences and stories helped create the customer scenarios that open each chapter as well as the hundreds of tips, techniques, and examples that appear. We thank them for partnering with us in the development of *Multicultural Customer Service: Providing Outstanding Service Across Cultures*.

We would also like to acknowledge the individuals who gave so freely of their time and multicultural expertise to critique the manuscript and suggest improvements. They include: Robin Johnson, Xie Ku, Susan Marcus-Owens, Susan Pecuh, and Marta Sanchez.

Special thanks to our editor, Carla Tishler. She was patient and supportive and made writing this book a tremendous learning experience.

Lastly, we want to acknowledge the important role of our partners, Dan Stokes and Frank Aguilar. They have always supported and encouraged our commitment to create a world where people work together and serve each other with caring and respect.

CONTENTS

Chapter 7   87

Communicating across Language Differences

Chapter 8   101

Multicultural Customer Service: Service Examples and Heroes

Self-Assessment

As a customer service representative, you are already serving a variety of customers with various needs. As you begin to work through this book, you will gain additional concepts and skills for serving your multicultural customers. Take a moment to assess your current level of skill and understanding. With this information, you can focus on strengthening some areas while continuing to build others.

You can determine the extent of your multicultural customer service knowledge and skills, by giving yourself a 3 for each *Almost Always*, a 2 for each *Sometimes*, and a 1 for each *Almost Never*.

	Almost Always	Sometimes	Almost Never
1. I understand that providing quality customer service to all of my customers is a part of my job.	_____	_____	_____
2. I understand that quality service is ultimately determined by the person who receives the service.	_____	_____	_____
3. I know that when I provide meaningful, individual service, I, my company, and my customers benefit.	_____	_____	_____
4. I reach higher levels of customer service by adapting my style and approach, rather than providing *one-size-fits-all* service.	_____	_____	_____
5. I am aware of my own multicultural customer service knowledge, comfort level, and skills.	_____	_____	_____
6. I work to overcome the barriers that detract from my ability to deliver quality customer service.	_____	_____	_____
7. I understand how cultural values and expectations affect interactions between me and my customers.	_____	_____	_____
8. I believe that *different* does not mean *deficient*.	_____	_____	_____
9. I have some knowledge of other cultures.	_____	_____	_____

	Almost Always	Sometimes	Almost Never
10. I can move past my stereotypes to avoid misunderstandings and provide meaningful service.	_____	_____	_____
11. I determine and respond to the needs of my multicultural customers.	_____	_____	_____
12. I adapt my own manner of speaking and listening to communicate more effectively with my multilingual customers.	_____	_____	_____
13. I am careful not to interpret nonverbal behavior based only on meanings from my culture.	_____	_____	_____
14. I enjoy the differences I see in my customers.	_____	_____	_____
15. I genuinely desire to provide outstanding service to all my customers.	_____	_____	_____

DIRECTIONS: Take a moment now to total your responses in each column and then combine the scores for a grand total. Next, apply the grand total to one of the categories listed below. The category that reflects your score is an indicator of your current level of skills, knowledge and desire. A more complete indicator could be gained by asking your coworkers, supervisor and customers.

TOTAL _____ TOTAL _____ TOTAL _____

GRAND TOTAL _____

45–41   You believe you are providing for the needs of your multicultural customers.

40–31   You are well on your way to meeting your multicultural customers' needs.

30–19   You are gaining the knowledge and skills to meet each of your customer's individual needs.

Below 19   You are probably serving your customers in a one-size-fits-all style and your overall quality of service is probably suffering.

By participating in the remaining pages, you can build your knowledge and skills to increase the level of customer service you provide to all of your customers.

Multicultural Customer Service

Providing Outstanding Service Across Cultures

1 | What Is Customer Service?

This chapter will help you to:

- Define good customer service.
- Identify why customer service is an important part of your job.
- Gain techniques for providing good customer service to all customers.

Consider the following scenarios:*

Tanisha, a cashier in a department store, assisted a shopper by taking time to answer questions and make suggestions on a clothing item. Surprised by the sincerity and helpfulness, the customer jokingly asked Tanisha if she was involved in the store's profit sharing. Tanisha smiled and said, "No, but the more clothes you buy and the happier you are with our products and services, the more hours I get to work!" ∎

■ Think about It

How does this employee view her job? Her customers? How do you think the customer felt after meeting the store cashier? _____

_____

_____

_____

_____

_____

_____

*Comments about these scenarios are found in Appendix A.

A hospital was striving to share the importance of customer service with all employees. Each week during New Employee Orientation, the CEO discussed her commitment to customers and to customer service. During this week's orientation session, a new graduate nurse in the back of the room spoke up and declared, "I am not here to serve anyone!" ■

How did this employee view the job? The customers? How might the customers feel after encountering this employee? _____

_____

_____

You may wonder if serving customers is a part of your job? After all, cashiers were hired to receive payments, waiters hired to serve food, housekeepers hired to clean rooms, car rental agents to rent cars, and nurses to distribute medications. Right?

But what if cashiers saw their jobs as assisting waiting customers, or car rental agents saw themselves as transportation providers for families and business travelers, and healthcare providers saw themselves as caregivers for people and their families? What impact would this way of viewing each of these jobs have on customer service, on the people who provide the service, and on the customers themselves?

Today, all organizations and all employees are in the customer service business. Take a moment now to look at your job and the customer service you provide.

CUSTOMER SERVICE AS PART OF YOUR JOB

■ **T i m e   O u t**

Consider the following questions to determine how your job includes service. You may be surprised to realize just how many of your responsibilities are focused on and around customers.

What is my job? _____

My major duties are:

_____

_____

_____

_____

I provide the following services to customers:

_____   _____   _____

_____   _____   _____

_____   _____   _____

_____ percent of my job involves working with customers? (Or, how many hours each day do I spend working with or for customers?)

What knowledge, skills, or training do I have?

_____   _____   _____

_____   _____   _____

_____   _____   _____

What knowledge, skills, or training do I need? _____

_____

_____

WHAT IS GOOD CUSTOMER SERVICE?

Good customer service differs from providing the product the customer requests. It is the way, method, or approach that is used that creates a positive feeling or experience for the customer. Providing good customer service is an art form.

Here is an example: Imagine that your job is to provide parts at an automobile parts store. **What** you do is provide quality car parts to people

1

in need of car repair. **How** you deliver that product (quality car parts) is customer service. To begin you smile and acknowledge the customer by saying something like, "Good morning. How can I help you today?" You work to understand his or her needs by listening and then by asking clarifying questions. You have an understanding of your products so you can explain different choices, and then provide the necessary part. You remember to really appreciate and thank the customer for the business and do this in a pleasant, respectful manner, focusing on the individual customer and his or her needs.

Customer service can seem intangible and can be difficult to give. Most organizations advertise that they believe in quality service and most service providers say they provide it. But, *what is good service?* Generally, good service means meeting your customers' needs in ways that have value and meaning to them. Customers experience you and your service one moment at a time. This means one meal, one car repair, one checkout line experience at a time. Each moment that the customer is being served by you is a "moment of truth" for that customer. Each customer experience or moment of truth determines whether the customer will return to do business with you again and what the customer will tell others about your organization and your service.

Customer service means something different to each person, but ultimately good service is determined by the customer who is the recipient of your service. Because each person's needs and situation are different, customer service is never "one size fits all." Each moment must be focused on and each service encounter tailored for that one individual. You know what good service is because it feels good when you receive it, just as you know when you have received poor service.

Think about It

Your Customer Service Experience

Answer the following questions from the perspective of a customer and then from the perspective of a service provider.

1

As a customer:

1. Think of a time when you experienced what you considered to be good customer service. Where were you? What was the situation?

_____

_____

What did the service provider do or say that created that feeling of good service for you?

_____

_____

2. Now think of a time when you asked for or needed something out of the ordinary. Where were you? What was the situation? _____

_____

_____

Did the organization or the service provider meet your need? _____

Was more done than expected? _____

_____

If so, how? _____

What feeling(s) did you leave with? _____

_____

As a service provider:

3. Think of a time when you had what you considered to be an unusual request from a customer. What was the situation? _____

_____

How did you work with the customer? What did you do or say?

_____

_____

1

Did you go beyond what was expected? _____ If so, how? _____

_____

How would you rate the customer's level of satisfaction? _____

As you consider the time and energy you spend serving customers, would you say that you are providing good service? _____ How do you know? _____

What do customers say to others about your service? What do you want them to say? _____

What feeling(s) do you want them to leave with? _____

WHY IS PROVIDING GOOD SERVICE IMPORTANT?

We all realize that if we don't serve customers, satisfy their needs, and deliver a quality product, we won't have a business or a job! Most employees understand the importance of customer satisfaction and how customers add to the success of the business and to their personal success. Providing the kind of service that meets individual needs and adds value to each customer's experience makes customers feel:

- Valued.
- Respected.
- Heard.
- That they received a quality product or service.

Customer service is important to customers and to organizations. Building the knowledge and skills to provide meaningful, individual service to all your customers will benefit you as well. It will:

- Give you ways to meet your customers' needs and requests.
- Reduce your stress.

- Increase your job satisfaction.
- Give you valuable, marketable skills.
- Make your organization more successful so that you can continue working.
- Increase the pride you feel in yourself and in the work that you do.

CONSIDER YOUR CUSTOMER SERVICE IMPACT

Supervisors and employees have responsibilities to their organizations for controlling costs and increasing revenue. Almost all employees in today's economy have an idea of costs and profits and how customers are tied to the bottom line.

Take a moment to consider the financial impact of the quality of service you provide to your customers.

Gains

Analyze what your organization would gain if just one of your customers buys the product or is satisfied with your service.

1. How much does one customer usually spend if they buy your service or product?

$_____

2. What if the customer continues to return for the next year? Say once each month?

$_____ × 12 months $_____

How about over a lifetime, say the next 20 to 30 years? How much money would that customer have spent with your organization?

$_____

3. How many customers like this do you serve each day? _____

   Each month?   _____

   Each year?   _____

4. What, then, is the total of gained revenue? _____

5. What does that mean to you in your job? _____

_____

_____

Losses

Now analyze the impact of lost business. Think of a time when you received poor customer service. Did you purchase the product or service? Did you return to do business again? How many people did you tell about your experience?

1. Consider the cost of an average product or service that you provide.

$\$$_____

2. What if the customer continues to return for the next year, say, once each month?

$\$$_____ × 12 months $\$$_____

How about over a lifetime, say the next 20 to 30 years? How much money would that customer have spent with you?

$\$$_____

3. Now, multiply the above amount by 10. That is the number of people that an unhappy customer tells about poor treatment!

$\$$_____

It is easy to see what this loss can mean to your job and to the financial stability of the organization.

1

TECHNIQUES FOR PROVIDING GOOD CUSTOMER SERVICE

Each time you interact with your customers you have an opportunity to provide good service. All customers have certain basic expectations when they conduct their business with you. They expect customer service providers to:

- Provide the product and service for which they came.
- Provide that service in a way that is respectful and meaningful.
- Assist in solving problems and accomplishing their business.
- Apologize when something goes wrong and make it right.

How well you meet the customer's basic expectations in a way that each customer appreciates will determine each customer's level of satisfaction. In addition to providing the product or service that the customer requests, the following general techniques will contribute to customers' satisfaction.

Technique 1: Be Aware That Your Customer Needs Your Attention

Stay focused and look for signs that your customer needs attention. Be ready—physically and mentally—to serve them. When a customer calls or enters your area, stop what you are doing, look at the customer, and ask how you can help: "Good Morning! How may I assist you?" or "Hi! How can I help you today?" If you are busy assisting someone else, you can acknowledge the customer by saying, "Just one moment, please," or "I will be with you in just one moment."

Technique 2: Listen To Understand

Listen to your customers in a way that lets them know that you are really trying to understand their needs. Listen with the intent to understand, rather than to formulate an immediate reply. Sometimes it is easier if you

1

consider how people would feel after a long flight, driving through a new town, dealing with unfamiliar policies and rules, or not understanding the customs and language. It is easy to assume that we know everything we need to know about our customer's needs, but until we ask and sincerely listen, we may be missing some important clues and techniques for satisfying the customer in ways that are meaningful to him or her.

As you are listening to the customer, consider:

- What situation is the customer describing?
- What is important to the customer in this situation?
- What obstacles or disappointments is or has the customer experienced?
- What is she/he asking for?
- What alternatives/solutions do I have?
- Do I really understand?

Remember, before suggesting solutions, let the customer know you have heard the question, concern, or request and that you want to help. You may say, "Yes, I understand and I can help you," or "Yes, and it would be my pleasure to assist you."

Technique 3: Ask Questions To Gain Information

Once you understand the customer's request, ask clarifying questions to gain additional information or to clarify the request or situation. You can better ensure a helpful answer if you phrase the question in a way that is beneficial to the customer. You might say, "So that I can recommend a restaurant that you would like, tell me about the kind of food your family prefers." This kind of question tells the customer that you care about individual service. Open-ended questions like, "How familiar are you with our product?" give you an understanding of the customer's comfort level and lets you know what kind and how much additional information to offer.

Technique 4: Acknowledge When Things Go Wrong

When something goes wrong, it is important to let customers know that you understand their situation. Apologize and assure them you will work to make it right. Above all, follow through with your promise. For example, you might say, "I am sorry that your dinner was not warm enough! I will replace it right away."

Technique 5: Appreciate The Customer

Be sure to sincerely appreciate your customers and to thank them for their business or suggestions. This lets them know that you have enjoyed working with them and hope they will return. Simply and sincerely saying, "Thank you" or "Thanks for doing business with us today" is an effective way of appreciating the customer.

Technique 6: Serve All Customers As They Wish To Be Served

Realize that every customer, from every background, has individual needs and wants service delivered in a respectful, meaningful way. If the customer that you are working with seems similar to your previous customer, don't assume that customer's needs and expectations are the same. A good rule is "serve people as they wish to be served," rather than how you personally might like to receive the service. These are some of the basics of providing good customer service.

The following chapters will deal more specifically with tailoring customer service to make it more meaningful and valuable to all your multicultural customers.

Chapter 1 Checkpoints

✓ Each customer defines "good service" for herself.

✓ Customer service done well will meet your customers' needs, reduce your stress, increase your job satisfaction, provide you with valuable, marketable skills, and make your organization more successful.

✓ Six techniques for providing good customer service are:
- Be aware of your customer's need for attention.
- Listen to the customer completely.
- Ask questions to gain more information or to clarify the request, need, or situation.
- Acknowledge when things go wrong and work to correct the situation.
- Appreciate the customer.
- Serve all customers as they wish to be served.

2 | Providing Multicultural Customer Service

This chapter will help you to:

- Define multicultural customer service.
- Identify your multicultural customers.
- Explore the challenge of providing meaningful customer service across cultures.
- Identify benefits of providing excellent service across cultures.
- Enhance your multicultural customer service.

Consider this scenario:*

Robert is a receptionist in a doctor's office. As patients come into the office, they are required to sign in on a form on his desk. When he needs to speak to them or let them know that it is their turn, he calls to them using their first names. He has been told that using first names lets the customer know that this is a friendly doctor's office. Lately he has noticed that more names are becoming unusual and difficult to pronounce. And recently when he smiled and called a patient by his first name, the patient looked displeased and did not answer. ■

■ Think about It

How did Robert and the customer feel at the moment of truth? What could Robert have done differently to increase his level of service? _____

_____

---

*Comments about this scenario are found in Appendix A.

2

ADJUST YOUR DELIVERY

One way to improve your chances of providing positive experiences for your customers is to adapt your style and approach to meet the customer's needs and expectations. This is often referred to as adjusting your service delivery approach to fit each customer rather than treating all customers the same. In this way, your customers are likely to feel higher levels of satisfaction because they feel that you are providing a service designed especially for them.

Your job is made more complex when you serve customers who may represent many different cultures and therefore may have needs and expectations outside of the traditional ones you are accustomed to working with. Additional skills are needed if you want these customers to walk away feeling that you have been aware of their needs, listened to them, asked questions to gain additional information, and provided for their needs in a way that is meaningful to them.

WHAT IS MULTICULTURAL CUSTOMER SERVICE?

In Chapter 1, we defined good service as meeting customers' needs in ways that have value and meaning to them. Remember, it is the individual customer who determines if good service has been provided.

Multicultural customer service means understanding that a customer's needs and expectations may vary across cultures. In order to provide the same quality service to all of your customers, you can adapt your personal style and usual business practices to meet their needs—even when their request or approach may seem unusual to you. For example, Robert could easily adjust the way he addressed patients by adopting a more formal yet still friendly approach.

HOW IS MULTICULTURAL CUSTOMER SERVICE DIFFERENT?

What are some of the differences that must be considered when serving multicultural customers?

- Differences in customer expectations based on cultural differences.
- Differences based on individual and family values.
- Language differences.
- Protocol and courtesy differences.
- Differences in religious needs.
- Communication style differences:
    Verbal.
    Nonverbal.
- Differences in logistical needs:
    Currency.
    Transportation.
    Measurement systems and sizing.
- Differences in customs:
    Food.
    Holidays, rituals, and celebrations.
- Other.

Who Are Your Multicultural Customers?

Who are your U.S. customers and your international customers?

_____ Asian-Americans	_____ Hispanic-Americans
_____ Asians	_____ Africans
_____ Native Americans	_____ African-Americans
_____ Eastern Europeans	_____ Pacific Islanders
_____ Anglo-Americans	_____ Alaskans
_____ Western Europeans	_____ Caribbean Islanders

_____ Hawaiians and
Pacific Islanders

_____ Central Americans

_____ South Americans

_____ Australians

_____ Canadians

_____ Mexicans

_____ Middle Easterners

_____ Indians

_____ Others

This is just a glimpse of the diversity of customers today! Within each geographic region are many countries and cultural groups. For example, the Middle East is made up of more than 20 Arabic countries and Israel.

Within each country are many different cultural groups. Many other dimensions of diversity also influence individual customers, such as:

☐ Ethnic background

☐ Religion

☐ Physical abilities

☐ Gender

☐ Social class

☐ Vocation

☐ Family structure
and status

☐ Economic status

☐ Education

☐ Age

☐ Political beliefs

Individual customers may consider themselves part of several different ethnic and cultural groups. It is important to remember that while we are gaining some general knowledge about culture and multicultural customers, this information can serve as guidelines only. Every customer is an individual and will not fit perfectly into any broad statements about cultural groups.

■ **Think about It**

Why Is Delivering Outstanding Multicultural Customer Service Important?

Take a moment to choose the correct response.

1. Currently ethnic minority shoppers (predominantly African-Americans, Hispanic-Americans, and Asian-Americans) spend $_____ on consumer products.

   a. $500 million
   b. $500 billion
   c. $5 billion
   d. $50 billion

2. _____ Americans now count some language other than English as their primary language.

   a. 5 million
   b. 20 million
   c. 65 million
   d. 100 million

3. Ethnic dishes now comprise _____ percent of restaurant entrees.

   a. 5 percent
   b. 15 percent
   c. 30 percent
   d. 46 percent

4. According to the United States Travel and Tourism Administration, 45.5 million tourists from around the world traveled to the United States in 1994. Revenues for 1994 totaled:

   a. $70,000 (seventy thousand)
   b. $700,000,000 (seven hundred million)
   c. $77,000,000,000 (seventy-seven billion)

5. By the year 2000, _____ percent of all business travelers will be women.

   a. 25 percent
   b. 35 percent
   c. 50 percent
   d. 60 percent

2

6. It is projected that by the year 2040, the U.S. population will exceed 355 million. What percentage will be foreign born?

   a. 3 percent
   b. 9 percent
   c. 11 percent
   d. 14 percent

7. Do you know what your organization's customer base/profile is? If so, what is it?

_____

8. What changes are you seeing in the customers you serve?

_____

_____

_____

WHY STRIVE TO PROVIDE GOOD MULTICULTURAL CUSTOMER SERVICE?

There are many reasons to strive to improve customer service skills for multicultural customers. Besides the benefits to customers in increased comfort and satisfaction, there are benefits for you and your organization. Can you think of other benefits in addition to the ones listed below?

Benefits for You

- Increase your own personal and organizational effectiveness.
- Remain employed.
- Become more promotable.
- Increase job satisfaction.
- Reduce stress and frustration.

Quiz Answers: 1, B; 2, B; 3, C; 4, C; 5, C; 6, D.

- Expand your comfort zone and increase your knowledge of the world.
- Avoid embarrassment.
- Receive salary and gratuity increases.

Benefits for Your Organization

- Increase customer satisfaction leading to repeat customers.
- Increase personal and organizational effectiveness.
- Increase profitability due to ability to compete successfully.
- Reduce advertising/marketing costs due to increased word-of-mouth referrals.
- Attract new customers.

HOW TO GET STARTED

Once you have made the decision to enhance the quality of service you provide to your multicultural customers, why not get started today? Although culture is complex, many of the adaptations you can make to your customer service approach are quite simple.

Here are some multicultural customer service tips to get you started. You can also find many more tips, techniques, examples, and tools throughout this book.

1. Find out your customer's preferred way of being addressed and use it. Many organizations teach employees to find out the customer's name and use it. They also teach that using first names is a sign of friendliness. But this is not a "universal truth." Many customers from diverse groups prefer to be addressed by titles or by their last names. Use of first names can actually be insulting to some customers. Also consider which name to use. Does the surname (family name or last name) or the given name come first? What about customers with multiple names? Did you know some countries don't use last names?

With all the differences, how do you know how to address your customers? You can ask! For example, "How would you like me to address you?"

2. Pronounce names and titles correctly. Even if you have to ask several times how to pronounce a person's name or title, it's important to pronounce it correctly. In the opening scene, Robert was beginning to experience difficulty with names. Sometimes service providers have been heard to say, "That's too difficult for me. I'll call you _____ while you are here." They then substitute a familiar name for the customer's real name. This is disconcerting to the customer and does not show respect for his or her wishes.

3. Err on the side of formality. While informality feels natural to many of us, most cultural groups around the world value formality. To many people, formality in relationships demonstrates respect for the other person. It's usually a good rule of thumb to interact with customers in a slightly more formal or respectful way than we would act with our close friends.

4. Avoid assuming. It's easy to assume that others want to be greeted and treated just like we would want. In multicultural customer service, assumptions about the other person's needs, expectations, or behaviors are often incorrect. We will see later how different cultural values influence customer needs and behaviors.

Chapter 2 Checkpoints

✓ Customers have different expectations and needs.

✓ To reach high levels of customer service with all your customers, adapt your style and approach so that you never provide a one-size-fits-all service.

✓ Multicultural customer service means understanding that a customer's needs and expectations may vary across cultures.

✓ You can begin now to provide quality customer service to your multicultural customers by:
- Discovering your customer's preferred way of being addressed and using it.
- Pronouncing names and titles correctly.
- Erring on the side of formality.
- Avoiding making assumptions.

3 | Developing Cultural Understanding

This chapter will help you to:

- Gain a general understanding of culture.
- Understand how cultural values and expectations affect the interaction between the customer service provider and the customer.
- Recognize stereotypes about cultural groups and use a process for moving past stereotypes.

Consider the following situation.*

A large delegation of Japanese businessmen arrive in the hotel's third-floor lobby for check-in. The front desk clerk, Regina, assists the guests and assigns them to rooms on the second, fifth, and sixth floors. Regina directs the guests to take the elevator up to the fifth and sixth floor and to the escalator down to the second floor.

Regina learns a few minutes later from the front-desk manager that the men are displeased with their rooms. Their group coordinator has called and asked the front-desk manager to upgrade those on the second floor to better rooms. Regina checks the system and finds that there are no more rooms on the fifth or sixth floors, although there are empty rooms on the twelfth floor. She decides not to move the guests—the twelfth floor would be no closer for the guests to their associates, and besides, all the rooms are pretty much the same. ■

---

*Comments about this scenario are found in Appendix A.

■ **T h i n k   a b o u t   I t**

Why might the customers be displeased with their rooms? What could Regina do to help meet the customers' expectations and needs? What cultural information might be helpful to her?

3

WHAT IS CULTURE?

To better understand how to serve our multicultural customers, we need a basic awareness of culture and how it shapes people and guides their interactions with others. Here is a brief description of culture:

- Culture is the total way of life of a group of people.
- Culture is a set of rules—both written and unwritten—by which people live. It's the "way things are done around here." Rules include laws, policies, customs, habits, behavioral guidelines, and etiquette.
- Every group develops its own culture over time. For example, there are national, regional, ethnic, religious, gender, organizational, and family cultures.
- We're often not aware of the influence of our own culture until we leave it and become immersed in another culture.
- Culture is learned. The older members in the culture (parents, teachers, religious leaders, role models, writers, etc.) pass on their beliefs and behaviors to the younger members.
- Culture structures our perception of the world and defines what is considered "common sense" and what is acceptable behavior.
- Culture is complex.

FIFTY WAYS CULTURE INFLUENCES US

Culture affects every aspect of a person's life. Here is a list of 50 ways culture influences people.

Etiquette and Behavior

- How we greet each other.
- What's considered common courtesy.
- What's considered impolite.
- How we show respect and disrespect.
- What is embarrassing.
- What makes us feel good.
- What we eat and how we eat.
- What we wear.
- What we buy and how we behave in stores.
- How often we touch each other and how we touch each other.
- How closely we stand next to each other.
- The holidays we celebrate and the way we celebrate.
- How we use money, credit, and bartering.
- What is risqué.
- How we seek and use health services.
- What we find humorous.
- How we use mass transit.
- Seating placement in a room.

Beliefs and Values

- What is beautiful or ugly.
- What are worthwhile goals in life.
- The nature of God and other religious beliefs.
- Whether a person is in control of his or her own life or whether fate determines one's life.
- Common sense.
- Our perceived needs.
- Whether privacy is desirable or undesirable.
- Appropriate health care.
- Appropriate personal hygiene.

3

3

Communication

- The language we speak.
- What should be said; what should be left unsaid.
- What is appropriate "small talk."
- Whom we speak to; to whom we should not speak.
- Whether communication should be direct or indirect.
- Whether conversation should be formal or informal.
- The meaning of hand gestures, facial expressions, and other nonverbal communication.
- How often we smile, whom we smile at, and the meaning of a smile.

Human Relations

- The role of the individual.
- The roles of men and how men should behave.
- The roles of women and how women should behave.
- The importance of harmony in a group.
- The importance of competition between individuals.
- Social class system.
- Hierarchy in business relationships.
- Interactions between strangers.
- How to interact with a person in authority (boss, police officer, teacher, etc.).
- How to interact with a person who is serving us.
- Relationships and obligations between friends.
- Relationships and obligations between parents and children and other family members.
- Crowd or audience behavior.

Time

- How time is scheduled and used.
- Whether schedules are important or unimportant.
- The importance of maintaining tradition.
- The importance of preparing for the future.
- Whether old age is valuable or undesirable.

We've listed 50 ways culture influences people. In other words, these are ways culture affects customers and customer service providers. In the scenario at the beginning of the chapter, we saw that customers have expectations and behave in certain ways based on their culture. The following are a few more examples of how cultural differences affect customer service:

- In the United States, tour operators and convention planners usually schedule free time in an itinerary. This allows for independent activities and individual privacy, which are highly valued by many participants. However, there are cultural groups that prefer not to have unstructured free time in an itinerary. To them, group activities are considered more desirable and a better use of time. A well-planned itinerary would provide several structured small-group activities from which to choose during the free time.

- Shopping etiquette and behavior are different in stores around the world. In U.S. department stores, it's common for shoppers to browse around on their own, touch the merchandise, and try on clothing to see if they like it. There is no obligation to purchase, regardless of how many items are scrutinized or tried on. If they purchase an article and then change their mind, they often expect to be able to return it for a refund. Shoppers generally don't expect to bargain or barter and often will pay with credit card or check, rather than with cash.

- In some cultures, shoppers are accustomed to the clerk assisting them in the selection of merchandise. This includes picking out fruits and vegetables in a market or merchandise in a store. Touching the merchandise is impolite. Trying on clothing without buying anything or returning items for refund are also considered inappropriate. In some cultures, paying with cash even for very expensive items and bargaining and bartering are common.

Think about It

From your experiences, what other aspects of culture and how culture influences people come to mind? Think about groups you have been a part of, places you have traveled or lived, and customers you have served.

_____

_____

_____

_____

LEARNING ABOUT CULTURAL VALUES AND BEHAVIORS

One of the most important things we learn from our culture is a set of values. By "values," we mean internal guidelines and benefits about what is important, right, or desired behavior. Learning about the underlying values of a culture and what's considered appropriate behavior will help you to:

- Better understand your customers' service expectations and needs.
- Understand behavior without judging it as wrong or inferior.
- Choose behavior that is sensitive (or at least not insulting) to your customers.

■ Think about It

My Cultural Values

Read each set of paired sentences regarding beliefs and behaviors. Circle the statement from each pair that most closely represents your beliefs and your behavior.

I believe . . .

All people are basically equal and should be treated the same.	People should be treated differently according to their place in society.

I believe . . .

Each person is responsible for his own life.	Fate determines life. People who take fate into their own hands are tempting fate or God.
It's best not to be dependent on others or have others depend on you.	It's best to be dependent on others and have others be dependent on you.
An individual should express her opinion even if it is in opposition to the beliefs of others in the group.	It's more important to maintain group harmony than for an individual in the group to express personal opinions.
New ideas and new ways of doing things are usually beneficial.	Tradition should be maintained unless there is sufficient reason to abandon tradition.
It's important to plan for the future.	It's important to look back through history as a guide for today.
Informal relationships and behavior between people are most comfortable.	Formal relationships and behavior between people are most comfortable.
Schedules should be established and maintained. Punctuality is important.	Schedules are flexible and less important than people and events. Things will happen when they should.
Individual reward, recognition, and attention are appreciated.	Individual reward, recognition, and attention are inappropriate and embarrassing to an individual and the group he is part of.

 T h i n k   a b o u t   I t

What Are My Customer Service Assumptions?

Read each pair of statements about customer service. Circle the one that most closely reflects your beliefs and assumptions about customers and customer service.

I believe . . .

Calling people by their first names is a sign of friendliness.	Calling people by their first names is a sign of disrespect.
Individuals generally wish to speak to their physicians, counselors, or clergy members in private.	Individuals generally wish to have their family members or community elder present when speaking about private matters with their physician, counselor, or clergy member.

I believe . . .

Customers entering a store are free to browse around, touch the merchandise, and try out/try on several different items even if they are not planning a specific purchase.

Customers entering a store should know what they wish to purchase, should inform the clerk, and should wait for the clerk to select the merchandise.

It's generally best to leave some free time in group itineraries so that individuals can have some time to do things on their own.

It's generally undesirable to schedule unstructured free time in a group itinerary.

It's appropriate to point out a customer's mistake in order to help the customer correct it.

It's inappropriate to point out a customer's mistake as it would cause the customer to lose face.

It's helpful to point out the customer service provider's mistake or unsatisfactory service so that it can be corrected.

It's inappropriate to point out a mistake made by the service provider as it would cause him to lose face.

Customers and the people serving them are equals and should treat each other accordingly.

Customers and the people serving them are often of different social classes and should treat each other accordingly.

Customer service providers are free to address any person in the customer group.

There are definite rules about who should speak to whom based upon age, gender, and hierarchy within the group.

Customers generally appreciate informality (e.g. self-service, relaxed environment, informal behavior). It's a sign that people are comfortable.

Customers generally appreciate formality (e.g. ceremonies, formal protocol and dress, seating arrangements). It's a sign of respect between people.

Service providers should smile and make friendly conversation with the customer.

Customer service providers should be reserved and respectful toward the customer.

Customers should be served on a first-come, first-serve basis.

Older, richer, or male customers should be served first.

APPRECIATING DIFFERENCES

For each statement you circled on the previous pages, you identified an individual belief or behavior. Individual beliefs and behaviors are not formed in a vacuum; they are influenced by the culture you grow up in. If you were raised in the United States, there's a good chance the statements on the left felt more comfortable to you. That's because these statements represent the American "norm" or most widely held beliefs or behaviors.

Of course you may have chosen some of the right-hand statements due to individual differences. That's why it's impossible to ever make a descriptive statement that is true for all people in a group.

Take a moment to reread the statements on the right. These phrases represent beliefs and behaviors that are widely held in some other cultures of the world. These beliefs and behaviors may seem odd to an American encountering them for the first time. In reality they are no more odd or unusual than our beliefs and behaviors are to others who encounter us for the first time.

Cultural differences are fascinating, but sometimes new and scary. The most important ingredient for learning about cultural differences and for serving multicultural customers is a sincere interest in other people and a respect for people who are different from you. If you demonstrate this respect, customers will appreciate your efforts, even if you make cultural mistakes.

Sadly, many people believe that "different" means "deficient" or "less valuable." Often when we look at other cultures that we don't understand, we begin to make judgments about the differences we see. Judgmental beliefs about a whole group of people are called stereotypes. Stereotypes can become a barrier between us and our customers. Consequently, it's important to learn to recognize our individual stereotypes so that we can move past them to provide excellent service to all of our customers—those who speak our language and share similar customs and dress, as well as those who don't.

> **CAUTION!** Two dangerous mistakes often made in multicultural learning are:
>
> 1. **Ethnocentrism**—Believing our own beliefs and behavior are superior or the only right ones:
>
> $$\text{Different} \neq \text{Deficient}$$
> $$\text{Different} = \text{Different}$$
>
> 2. **Stereotyping**—Believing that all people in a group are alike and leaving no room for individual differences

STEREOTYPES

Stereotypes are simple statements made about a whole group of people. For example,

"Tourists are _____   _____

_____   _____

_____   _____

What words first came to mind? Write down six stereotypes you know exist about tourists. You may not hold these stereotypes yourself but you know they exist. While as individuals, we may try not to stereotype people, stereotypes are so common in society that it's impossible to escape them.

How to Recognize Stereotypes

Use the following "stereotype test" to check for stereotypical statements, behavior, and thoughts.

Do I . . .

- Categorize whole groups of people together without regard for the individual?
  ("Teenagers are lazy." "All African-Americans are good in sports.")

- Describe or depict individuals in stereotypical terms?
  ("You know how women are." Stereotypical portrayal in movies of Latinos, Asians, and Native Americans in demeaning roles.)

- Consider individuals as exceptions to the rule if they do not fit my stereotype?
  ("He's really sensitive for a man." "You're not like other Jewish people." "You're OK for a woman.")

- Deny individuality to a person because his behavior doesn't fit my stereotype of group behavior?
  ("Why are you doing that? I thought Asians were supposed to be soft-spoken." "Old people shouldn't behave like that.")

- Label or judge behavior rather than describe it and seek to understand it?
  ("Brazilians are rude and pushy." "Americans are shallow.")

- Expect an individual to be a spokesperson for everyone in a group?
  ("Sam, what do gay men think about this?")

"Truths" about Stereotypes

- They exist. They are part of the information we receive from society.

- Most stereotypes contain a judgment about the group being stereotyped. (The judgment—good or bad, right or wrong, normal or abnormal—describes how the holder of the stereotype feels more than the actual behavior of the person being stereotyped.)

- Stereotypes are harmful to the person being stereotyped because they box the person in and don't allow any room for individuality.

- Stereotypes are harmful to the person holding them because they often color or distort information.
- Stereotypes are internal thoughts and beliefs that can be externalized through the words we choose and the behavior we use when we interact with others.

◼ Think about It

How Stereotypes Can Affect Customer Service

Review the three situations and answer the questions that follow.*

Craig, a sales representative, is representing his manufacturing company at a large trade show. His company is hoping to export its products to Asia in the future. A large international audience is expected at the show. In preparation for the trade show, Craig read several books about international business and cultural sensitivity. He read about the importance of business cards to the Japanese, so he had some of his business cards printed in Japanese on the reverse side.

On the day of the trade show, many attendees stop by his display to pick up information and his card. Craig gives his Japanese card to anyone who looks Asian and points out that the information is available in their language on the back of the card. ◼

What are the stereotypes at play? How do you think the Asian customers feel after meeting Craig? What would you recommend to Craig?

_____

_____

_____

_____

_____

*Comments about these scenarios are found in Appendix A.

Two customers enter a jewelry store and begin looking at the displays. One customer is a white male; the other customer is a black female. The sales representative, Joanne, approaches the white man and assists him. When he selects a piece of jewelry, she asks him, "How would you like to pay for this? Cash or credit?" A few moments later Joanne assists the black female customer who makes a similar selection. Joanne asks the customer, "Would you like to put this on layaway?" ■

3

What are the subtle stereotypes at play? How have Joanne's stereotypes affected her customer service for these two customers? Do you think Joanne is aware of the difference in the way she treated the two customers? Do the customers notice the difference?

_____

_____

_____

_____

_____

_____

Tomica, a new accounts representative at a local bank, knows many of her regular customers. Recently she has noticed that more young people are coming in to open checking accounts. Although Tomica has a list of products and services that she usually offers to her regular customers, she believes it is a waste of time to run through the list with people who look too young to care about many of the services such as safety deposit boxes and investment instruments. So, to save time with younger customers she provides only the services they ask for. ■

What are the stereotypes at play? What impact do Tomica's stereotypes have on the customer, on Tomica, and on the organization?

_____

_____

_____

3

_____

_____

_____

Identify three cultural or ethnic groups represented in your customer base. Identify stereotypes that exist about these customers. Record ideas to help you or your co-workers move past stereotypes to provide consistently high levels of service to all of your customers. You may wish to review your comments with a co-worker.

_____

_____

_____

_____

_____

_____

_____

_____

_____

Moving Past Stereotypes

Although stereotypes are widespread, there are ways to move past them.

1. Learn to recognize stereotypes. Acknowledge that stereotypes exist. Work to discover any stereotypes you have internalized about customers. Once you bring the stereotypes to conscious awareness, it's easier to choose behavior that is respectful of customers. However, if stereotypes remain in the subconscious level, we may act on them without even knowing it.

2. Remove judgments; describe behaviors. Remove the judgment words (for example, "Brazilians are pushy" or "Germans are cold"). Instead, describe the behaviors in factual ways. By looking at differences in Brazilian, American, and German behaviors, we can remove the judgments "pushy" and "cold" and make the following statements about behaviors. For example, one behavioral difference is how we use space.

"Many Brazilians stand more closely together than many Americans tend to do."
"Many Germans stand further apart than many Americans do."
(Many Brazilians maintain about one to two feet of personal space between them; Americans often maintain two to three feet of space between them. Germans tend to stand three or more feet apart when speaking together.)

3. Choose behavior that enhances relationships. If you view a customer as pushy or cold, you may be less willing to assist that customer. However, if you simply acknowledge the behavioral differences without believing that different means deficient, you free yourself to choose respectful, outstanding service behaviors for all customers.

Chapter 3 Checkpoints

✓ Culture influences all aspects of a person's behavior, beliefs, and expectations.

✓ It's important to remember that for every widely held cultural belief or behavior, there are individual differences among people.

✓ When we see cultural behaviors we do not understand, it's easy to judge the behavior as wrong or abnormal.

✓ *Different* simply means *different*. It does not mean *deficient*.

✓ Understanding other cultures makes it easier to move past stereotypes, avoid misunderstandings, and provide customer service that is meaningful to all of our customers

4 | Overcoming Barriers to Multicultural Customer Service

This chapter will help you to:

- Identify the barriers that get in the way of providing exceptional multicultural customer service.
- Assess your own multicultural customer service attitudes, knowledge, and skills.
- Gain ideas for expanding your multicultural "comfort zone."

Consider the following situation:*

Kathy is responsible for planning and coordinating a banquet honoring several of her firm's prestigious clients. Several hundred guests from across the community are expected to attend. The caterer has recommended a menu offering two appetizers (scallops wrapped in bacon and spinach-wrapped shrimp) followed by a choice of entrées including beef medallions, whole Maine lobster, and fettucini à la Carbonara. ■

■ **Think about It**

Will this menu be acceptable to the guests? Which customer groups may be negatively affected? What should Kathy do? _____

_____

_____

_____

_____

_____
*Comments about this scenario are found in Appendix A.

BARRIERS TO DELIVERING QUALITY CUSTOMER SERVICE

4

Often service providers become frustrated trying to deliver quality customer service. There are many reasons why this happens. Some of the barriers that can detract from your ability to deliver quality customer service to all of your customers are described below.

The Product   The product you are delivering to the customer—the food, the show, the merchandise, the service—doesn't always meet the customer's expectations. The product may not appeal to a broad group of people. Perhaps it's not adaptable to the special requests of customers.

The Organization   Consider whether:

- You have a clear policy and mission on outstanding customer service.
- You have customer-friendly policies or rules.
- The supervisor is supporting your efforts.
- Outstanding service is expected or rewarded.
- You are encouraged to vary your customer service delivery to help different customers reach equal levels of satisfaction.
- Your work environment looks and feels customer-friendly.

An organization's policies and practices can serve as "enhancers," making it easier to provide outstanding multicultural customer service. On the other hand, some policies and practices can get in the way or detract from the ability to effectively meet customer needs.

The Service Provider   Some of the reasons for failing to provide outstanding customer service are personal. Perhaps you don't always feel you have the knowledge, experience, or skills to satisfy your customers. Occasionally, you may lose your desire to make the extra effort necessary to meet the needs of each individual customer. In the chapter-opening scenario, Kathy lacked knowledge and experience, but had great desire to help her customers.

The Customer   Sometimes the customer appears demanding, controlling, irritable, confused, or frustrated. Customers may be unclear or unsure about their expectations. They may be happy one minute and demanding the next.

Even the best customer service providers occasionally fall into the trap of thinking, "If the customer would just go away, everything would be fine." It's true that if the customers would go away, you would have no more customer service problems to overcome, because you would have no more customers. No matter how difficult the customer appears at the moment, the customer is *not* the barrier to overcome. Rather, the customer is a *participant* in the customer service transaction. If you and the customer work together to meet that customer's needs, almost all other barriers can be overcome.

All of these—product, organizational policies and practices, you as the customer service provider, and the customer—affect customer service. You may have limited control over product development, organizational policies, or the customer's behavior, but you can control how well you handle the customer conversation and provide the service. Customer service is an art that requires commitment and many skills. Multicultural customer service requires an even greater skill level. These skills can be learned, practiced, and put into use on a daily basis.

■ Think about It

Identifying Barriers

Review the three customer service situations below and identify the barriers to providing excellent multicultural customer service. Does the customer service provider lack knowledge or skills? Is the product itself a barrier to customer satisfaction? Do the organizational policies make it harder to provide effective customer service to all customers?*

---

*Comments about these scenarios are found in Appendix A.

A customer approaches the information counter and begins to explain his request to the representative, Susan. The customer has a heavy accent. Susan interrupts and explains, "Maria speaks Spanish and will be happy to help you." Turning to Maria, she says, "Maria, will you help this man? He doesn't speak English very well." ■

Is this good customer service? What barriers can you identify? What can Susan do to improve the level of customer service being provided?

_____

_____

_____

_____

_____

_____

The policy in a well-known department store is to require a U.S. driver's license as identification when cashing a check. Rob, a sales representative, has followed the policy, refusing to accept checks from anyone who does not hold a U.S. driver's license. Several of the store's customers have complained that they are being treated unfairly. ■

Which customer groups could be negatively affected? Is this good customer service? How might these customers feel? What are your recommendations for Rob and for the store? _____

_____

_____

_____

_____

_____

Tina is the seating hostess in a family-style restaurant. A family entering the restaurant asks her if the restaurant has any entrées for vegetarians. Tina explains that all of the dishes contain meat or animal products. When they ask her to recommend a nearby restaurant serving vegetarian dishes, Tina says she doesn't know of any. ■

Is this good customer service? What barriers can you identify? What are your recommendations for Tina and for the restaurant? _____

_____

_____

_____

_____

_____

YOU MAKE THE DIFFERENCE

As seen in the previous examples, an organization's systems, policies, practices, or product can enhance or detract from customer service efforts. However, the focus of this book is on developing *your own individual knowledge and skills* for serving multicultural customers. The quality of your personal interactions with your customers is something within your own control. Successful customer interactions frequently depend on *you*, the customer service provider. The following exercises will help you to focus on your own multicultural customer service knowledge, comfort level, behaviors, and skills.

■ Think about It

Awareness

Review each statement. Mark your response: "Always/Yes," "Sometimes," "Rarely/No," or "I Don't Know."

	Always/Yes	Sometimes	Rarely/No	I Don't Know

Awareness

A. I am aware of:

1.   The multicultural customer service skills I possess.

2.   The multicultural customer service skills I need to develop.

3.   My own biases and stereotypes about customers.

4.   My personal pet peeves regarding customers.

B. I am comfortable with:

5.   Customers from other countries.

6.   Customers from ethnic groups different than my own.

7.   Older customers.

8.   Younger customers.

9.   Customers from the opposite gender.

10. Customers with different levels of education.

11. Customers with disabilities.

12. Customers who speak with an accent.

13. Customers with limited English abilities.

14. Customers who dress in an unusual style.

Behaviors

Review each statement. Mark your response: "Always/Yes," "Sometimes," "Rarely/No," or "I Don't Know." Think of previous customer interactions and give a specific behavioral example that supports your answer.

	Always/Yes	Sometimes	Rarely/No	I Don't Know

Behaviors

C. I:

1.   Accept differences among customers without becoming judgmental.

     Example:

	Always/Yes	Sometimes	Rarely/No	I Don't Know
2. Behave in a way that demon-strates I value and respect each customer. Example:	_____	_____	_____	_____
3. Challenge my first impression of customers; I'm willing to take a second look. Example:	_____	_____	_____	_____
4. Avoid making or supporting eth-nic, racial, or sexual slurs or jokes to or about customers. Example:	_____	_____	_____	_____
5. Refuse to participate in small talk about customers that reinforces bias and stereotypes. Example:	_____	_____	_____	_____
6. Am working to expand my own comfort level around customers whom I perceive as "different." Example:	_____	_____	_____	_____
7. Take the extra time that helping customers with unique needs may require. Example:	_____	_____	_____	_____
8. Respect the customer's cultural differences. Example:	_____	_____	_____	_____
9. Find out how customers would like to be addressed and use that form of address. Example:	_____	_____	_____	_____
10. Make an effort to pronounce cus-tomers' names and/or titles cor-rectly. Example:	_____	_____	_____	_____
11. Adapt my own speaking style to communicate more effectively with customers who have limited English skills. Example:	_____	_____	_____	_____
12. Improve my listening in order to communicate more effectively with customers who have limited English skills. Example:	_____	_____	_____	_____

4

	Always/Yes	Sometimes	Rarely/No	I Don't Know
13. Offer additional information or assistance to customers who are from out of town or out of the country, or who may be unfamiliar with this area or its customs. Example:	_____	_____	_____	_____
14. Welcome each and every customer regardless of age, nationality, language, communication style, personality, appearance, abilities, or disabilities. Example:	_____	_____	_____	_____
15. Try to listen fully and learn from customers who have expressed dissatisfaction with my/our customer service. Example:	_____	_____	_____	_____

PERSONAL BARRIERS

As we saw earlier, *you* make the difference. It's up to you to overcome any *personal* barriers to offering excellent multicultural customer service. One barrier we have already discussed is stereotypes. A second barrier to overcome is personal *pet peeves*.

What Is a Pet Peeve?

A pet peeve is an emotional hot button that causes you to have a quick, strong reaction to a particular word, behavior, or personality. For example, if you have a pet peeve about people who stand very close to you, you might respond to a customer who steps up into your personal space by moving away and grimacing.

■ Think about It

Take a moment to identify several of your personal pet peeves. Then indicate how you might automatically respond to a customer who has the behavior you find irritating.

Pet Peeve   Your Response

_____   _____

_____   _____

_____   _____

_____

Food for Thought.   If a customer makes you uncomfortable or gets on your nerves, are you more likely to:

- Try to complete the service as quickly as possible?
- Lower the level of customer service you provide?
- Respond to the customer in a rude or abrupt way?

In multicultural customer interactions, monitoring your response is very important. Most behaviors are culturally learned. What is considered acceptable behavior varies from culture to culture. Desirable behavior in your culture could actually be a pet peeve or even an insult to someone raised in a different culture. And vice versa—the customer's behavior, which may seem inappropriate or irritating to you, could actually be polite or desirable behavior in the home culture.

   Knowing your own pet peeves is essential for good customer service. By becoming aware of your reactions to pet peeve behaviors, you can choose the appropriate response to your customer rather than allowing pet peeves to become a barrier to excellent customer service.

Think about It

Identify Your Pet Peeves

Review the behaviors below. Circle those that represent any personal pet peeves that cause you to (over)react emotionally.

The following bothers me or distracts me:

People who:

- Speak very little.
- Talk a lot.
- Speak very softly.
- Speak in a very loud voice.
- Speak very vaguely.
- Are very direct and straightforward.
- Beat around the bush.
- Talk very slowly.
- Exaggerate.
- Stand very close to me.
- Stand far away from me.
- Touch me a lot.
- Never touch.
- Look away rather than make eye contact.
- Make very direct or intense eye contact.
- Have poor grammar.
- Speak with a heavy accent.
- Speak in a high-pitched voice.
- Don't speak English.
- Only speak when spoken to.
- Interrupt.
- Correct what I say.
- Directly challenge what I say.
- Criticize and critique.
- Agree with everything.
- Get very excited and animated when speaking.
- Remain calm and even-toned when speaking.
- Use a lot of large gestures.
- Use no gestures.
- Show no emotion in their facial expressions.
- Use formal words and behavior.
- Use slang or informal speech and behavior.
- Address me by my first name.
- Address me by my title or my last name.
- Insist that I address them by first name.
- Insist that I address them by last name or title.
- Smile a lot.
- Never smile.
- Point at me.
- Smell like body odor.
- Smell like perfume or deodorant.
- Wear a turban.
- Wear clothes or jewelry I consider inappropriate.
- Don't wait in line.

EXPANDING YOUR COMFORT ZONE

Most customer service providers report that there are some customers with whom they are very comfortable while other customers make them feel less comfortable. Often, at closer look, we discover that we are most comfortable with customers who:

- We perceive to be like ourselves.
- Communicate in a way that we are comfortable with.
- Have a need that we know how to address.

Think about It

Review your answers from Part B of the "Self-Awareness and Comfort Level" questionnaire . Identify one or two groups of customers with whom you would like to become more comfortable. _____

_____

_____

What might you do to enlarge your comfort zone so that it includes these customers?

_____

_____

Here are some more ideas for expanding your multicultural customer service comfort zone:

- Attend a training session on cultural awareness.
- Join a professional or social group where the membership is very diverse.
- Make friends with individuals from other ethnic groups and cultures.
- Attend a training session on multicultural customer service.

- Share ideas with co-workers about customer service.
- Learn a few greetings or phrases in the languages of your customers.
- Talk with customers about their customer service expectations and experiences.

Expanding your multicultural service comfort zone is continually rewarding—you will relate to so many more people and feel good doing it.

4

Chapter 4 Checkpoints

✓ The product, the organizational systems, policies and practices, the customer, and the service provider all affect the success of multicultural customer service.

✓ Outstanding multicultural customer service depends largely on you—the service provider.

✓ You *can* control your own multicultural customer service attitude, comfort level, knowledge, and skills.

✓ Identify and overcome your pet peeves so you can provide the best service possible.

✓ There are specific skills and behaviors associated with effective multicultural customer service. These behaviors and skills can be learned and practiced daily.

5 | Multicultural Customer Service Needs

This chapter will help you to:

- Identify special customer service needs of your multicultural customers.
- Build additional skills and resources for meeting these needs.

Consider the following situation.*

Carla is the customer service representative at a major rental car agency. She has been assisting quite a few international customers recently. Carla always follows standard procedures: When the customers arrive to pick up their rental car, she completes the paperwork, gives the car keys to the customers, and sends them out to the car lot to find their car. Carla was surprised to learn recently that several of her international customers have indicated that the car did not meet their expectations and that the rental experience was stressful. ■

■ Think about It

What could have gone wrong? What could Carla do differently in the future to increase the comfort and satisfaction level of her customers?

_____

_____

_____

_____

_____

*Comments about this scenario are found in Appendix A.

MEETING THE NEEDS OF THE MULTICULTURAL CUSTOMER

Providing outstanding multicultural customer service means meeting the needs of all customers, regardless of who they are and where they come from. In Chapters 2, 3, and 4, you began to explore how multicultural customers sometimes have different customer service needs and expectations based on cultural differences. This chapter helps you to anticipate and build skills for meeting the special needs of your diverse customers—one customer at a time.

Customers may be diverse in many ways. They may belong to a different ethnic group than your own. Some customers have health, age, family, religious, or lifestyle needs that are different than yours. Some may be recent immigrants who are still adjusting to life in America. You may also meet customers who are in the United States temporarily—international tourists and business people. Some may look, sound, and dress differently than you do.

When people travel outside of their own country, they encounter more daily challenges than they face at home. They may feel insecure about their personal security and ability to maneuver in the new location. They may interact with you, the service provider, in ways that are new to you or unexpected.

Recognizing the needs and expectations of each customer—whether from your own country or from elsewhere in the world—is an increasingly important skill. Practicing this skill will enable you to deliver your service in a way that's helpful and meaningful to each customer.

IDENTIFYING SPECIAL NEEDS

Meeting the special needs of your customers takes planning and empathy. The following questions will help you to put yourself in your customers' shoes. Answer these questions as a starting point to begin thinking about your customers' special needs.

Food

- Does my establishment offer a variety of food for customers with special dietary needs?
- Can the customers understand the menu?
- If special dietary requests are made, can we accommodate them? If not, can I refer customers to a location that can take care of their requests?

Religion

- Can customers meet their religious needs here?
- Where are services available for different religions?
- Am I respectful of different religious needs, customs, and attire?
- Do we consider religious holidays for religions other than our own in the scheduling and planning of events?

Money

- What types of currency or credit cards do we accept?
- Where is the closest foreign currency exchange service located?
- Do I know how to handle foreign currency exchange requests?

Language and Communication

- What percentage of my customers do not speak English?
- What are the most common foreign languages spoken by my clients?
- How can I help customers get their basic questions answered in their own language if they do not speak English?
- Am I willing and able to spend additional time with customers who have language barriers?
- What languages do I or my co-workers speak?

- What other language resources are available to my customers?
- Are written materials translated into the languages of our customers? Do these materials use words and measurements that are meaningful to them (e.g., Celsius temperature, kilometers)?
- Am I knowledgeable about communicating with customers with speech or hearing impairments?
- Where are TDDs (telecommunication devices for the deaf) located?

Health, Safety, and Security

- Are safety and security signs and emergency information translated into several languages?
- Where is the closest medical service with multilingual doctors or nurses?
- Do I accommodate customers with special medical needs willingly and fully?
- Are adaptors available for use with international appliances?

Shopping/Entertainment

- Do I understand the international size standards and can I help customers choose the correct American size?
- Do customers understand the return policy? Am I explaining it appropriately?
- Where can customers find foreign-language television, movies, or newspapers?

Transportation

- What types of public transportation are available? Can I explain them correctly to customers?
- Do I know how to locate wheelchair-accessible transportation?

- Are written travel directions and maps available to the most popular local destinations? Are these travel directions available in other languages?

Facilities/Services

- Are services, activities, and facilities available for different age groups?
- Are facilities of equal quality for users of different nationalities, ethnic groups, genders, and religions?

Service Delivery

- Do I approach all customers with equal enthusiasm and respect, regardless of how they are dressed or what they look like?
- Am I aware that my words and behaviors can be perceived by customers in ways I did not intend?

5

Think about It

How am I doing?

1. Think of at least two times in the past that you have had the opportunity to provide service to a customer with a special health or dietary need, a language barrier, a religious request, or any other special request based on her cultural or individual needs. List the situations below.

_____

_____

Were you able to anticipate her needs? Could you successfully resolve the customer's request?

_____

_____

_____

What would you do differently in the future? _____

_____

2. Next, consider these two important questions:
Does the service I currently provide meet the special needs of my multicultural customers? _____

_____

_____

Am I providing the service in a way that is comfortable for the customer, even if it stretches my own "comfort zone"? _____

_____

_____

3. Choose one or two questions listed in "Identifying Special Needs" on the previous pages that you would like to focus on to improve the quality of multicultural customer service you provide. Write down your initial thoughts on how to research the issues and respond to them.

Item One: _____

Ideas: _____

_____

Item Two: _____

Ideas: _____

_____

HOW TO DETERMINE AND RESPOND TO MULTICULTURAL CUSTOMERS' NEEDS

Each time we interact with customers, we have the opportunity to learn about customer expectations and needs. Many times we simply need to observe what difficulties they experience and listen to their questions and comments to find out. We can then work to help them *and* future customers overcome any customer service barriers we have discovered.

In addition, we can anticipate in advance special customer needs that may arise. Here are general guidelines to help you prepare to meet the needs of your multicultural customers.

1. **Describe how you typically help a customer:**
   - Key "Moments of Truth."
   - Product you deliver.
   - Information you provide.
   - Amount of time you spend with a customer during each "Moment of Truth."
   - Service delivery style.

2. **Identify the silent assumptions you make when you are presenting your service or product to a customer.** For example:
   - The customer has general knowledge and familiarity with our product.
   - The customer understands our process (how to get things done around here).
   - The customer will understand the language I am using.
   - The customer will be comfortable with my behavior.
   - Other assumptions.

3. **Check your assumptions to see if they are true for** *this individual customer.*
   - Ask questions about previous use of the product.
   - Recognize unfamiliarity with your product/process.
   - Listen for hesitation.
   - Check for comprehension. Does the customer have full fluency in English? Did I use technical jargon that anyone outside of my field or company would not understand?
   - Watch and listen for customer comfort with your style. Customers may perceive your behaviors to mean something other than what you intended.

5

- Seek additional information. Ask questions of customers. Learn from previous customer interactions. Read. Ask questions of co-workers or experts.

4. Determine how to adapt your customer service to meet the customer's needs.

- Consider whether additional information is needed.

- What adaptations can be made to the product?

- How should I adapt my customer service delivery style to meet the business and emotional needs of the customer?

We will look more closely at how to use these guidelines. The guidelines are broad suggestions that describe a process you can use with each customer. As a customer service provider, you must be flexible when using the guidelines. Bend them and enhance them to meet your customer's needs.

A Case Study

Using the four-step process just described, let's analyze the scenario of the rental car customer service representative, Carla, at the beginning of this chapter.

1. Describe how the representatives typically help the customer.

- Moments of Truth: Customer learns about the car agency, calls the reservation center to reserve a car, arrives at the airport, enters the car rental location, speaks with the customer service representative, completes paperwork, receives a car, leaves, and returns several days later to return the car.

- Product/service: Provide car or van for her business trip or vacation.

- Reservationist questions: Location of rental? Dates? Midsize car? Pickup at airport? Approximate time of pickup and return?

- Information provided: Cost; features (e.g., unlimited mileage); re-strictions (e.g., age); additional taxes, fees, or waivers; where to pick up vehicle.

- Amount of time reservationist spends with a customer is several minutes.
  Amount of time counter representative spends with customer: _____ minutes.

- Are the representatives able to spend additional time with the cus-tomer?

- Service delivery style: What words would Carla and her co-worker use to describe the manner in which they interact with customers?

2. Identify typical assumptions Carla and the reservationist made about the customer when presenting the service or product to the customers. They assumed:

- Customers were familiar with American cars and features and knew how to drive here.

- Customers were familiar with the car rental procedures.

- Customers understood the English language fully.

- "Quick and efficient" was a comfortable service style for the cus-tomers.

- If customers needed information, they would ask.

3. Check your assumptions to see if they are true for this indi-vidual customer. The following comments made by international cus-tomers who have rented a car in the United States show that individual customer needs and expectations are often *not* what we assume.

- "I was expecting a standard transmission. I wish the reservationist had warned us it was automatic."

- "The agent gave me the keys and told me to find my red Ciera. I'm unfamiliar with American cars and wandered around the lot for a long time."

5

- "At first we had a hard time learning to use the car. It took several hours before we realized the air conditioning could be adjusted. We were freezing. The cars are nice—but different."

- "Upon leaving the lot, I arrived at the first stoplight and stopped *right under* the light, as is customary in my country. We were nearly hit by other cars in the intersection. We soon learned that here the cars must stop about five meters *before* they arrive at the red light."

If both the reservationist and Carla had checked to see if their assumptions were true for each individual customer, they would have found that:

- Many international customers come from countries where the car brands, sizes, and features are different. Driving laws differ in each country as well.

- The rental car process can vary by country due to laws and local customs. As a result, the process may be unfamiliar to many.

- Many customers, particularly if in a foreign country or using a product for the first time, would like additional time and information. Some customers have never rented a car before and they don't know what questions to ask.

- Language differences can make comprehension for the customers difficult. Fatigue after long international flights makes it even harder to understand a foreign language.

4. Determine how to adapt the customer service to meet the customer's needs. What additional information can the reservationist and Carla provide to help the customers? They can:

- More fully explain car sizes and features rather than using the customary question "Midsize car?"

- Include information regarding automatic transmissions so that the customer will not be surprised.

- Offer a safety brochure that includes tips on driving in the United States.

Could the product be altered to meet the needs of the customer? In this case, yes. Carla's rental car agency offers manual transmission cars, but needs advance notice. By asking the customer to make this decision during the reservation process, this alteration could be made easily.

How can Carla and her co-worker alter their delivery style so that it meets the business and emotional needs of the individual customer? They can:

- Offer information that is important, even if it's not specifically requested.
- Ask questions such as, "Have you ever rented with us before? Are you familiar with driving in America?"
- Take additional time to answer questions and to provide information.
- Check for comprehension.

Note: Helpful techniques for communicating across language barriers are provided in Chapter 7.

Put It All Together

Next, use this four-step process to identify opportunities for adapting your own customer service to ensure equally high satisfaction for all of your customers. It's helpful to identify and focus on one customer interaction. You may choose to make extra copies of this page to use later.

Customer Interaction: _____

1. Describe how you typically help a customer.

_____
_____
_____
_____
_____

2. Identify typical assumptions you make about the customer when you are presenting your service or product.

_____

_____

_____

3. Check your assumptions to see if they are true for this individual customer.

_____

_____

_____

4. Determine how to adapt your customer service to meet the customer's needs.

_____

_____

_____

FINDING THE BALANCE

It's impossible to personally meet the needs of every customer. A restaurant may not be prepared to respond to a particular dietary need. Even if you learn one foreign language, the customer may speak another. A hotel may be too small to offer currency assistance. These are some examples of times when a customer's request may seem impossible to meet.

You may not always be able to offer the solution to your customer. *You can, however, offer the pathway to the solution.* This is what we call *finding the balance*—serving customers to the best of your abilities regardless of the limitations of your resources. In some cases, you may be able to satisfy your customer on your own. It other cases, you may decide that the best possible answer is "We can help you find someone who can do it for you." In either case, you'll be providing caring customer service.

By planning ahead, you can put together a team of service providers. Often, necessary resources for meeting the needs of your customers are available within your own company. Or, services may be provided free of charge within your local community. Knowing when and where to turn for help in order to assist your customers is one way to meet their needs in any situation. This approach will turn "we can't do it" into "we can help you" for many of your customer requests.

WHAT ARE YOUR RESOURCES?

Whether your multicultural customers are from your hometown or from around the world, meeting their needs and expectations may take some extra effort. You'll be better equipped to help your customers if you've prepared in advance.

Complete the following worksheet by locating one or two resources in your company or community for each customer need. You may wish to keep the completed worksheet in a visible place at work or discuss it in a staff meeting so that others can refer to it when helping customers.

Communication

Name the foreign languages most often spoken by your customers. ___

_____

_____

_____

Identify bilingual employees (with phone numbers) who are willing and able to assist with basic language needs. _____

_____

_____

_____

List two additional language resources (with phone numbers) in the community to help foreign-language customers. _____

_____

_____

_____

Identify where customers can find special communication services (e.g., TDDs, braille, large print information, foreign-language television, radio, and newspapers). _____

_____

_____

_____

List other important communication/language resources. _____

_____

_____

_____

Money

Locate the closest foreign-currency exchange office. List phone number, operating hours, travel directions, and general information. _____

_____

_____

_____

Food

Find out what special dietary requests nearby restaurants can accommodate. _____

_____

_____

_____

List the names and telephone numbers of several restaurants/caterers that are able to meet special dietary needs. _____

_____

_____

_____

Religion

Find out what religious holidays are celebrated by your employees and customers. Locate and post a multicultural calendar.* _____

_____

_____

Identify where information on various religious services can be obtained. Identify a quiet place for meditation for individuals seeking to practice their faith. _____

_____

_____

_____

5

Shopping

Locate and post equivalency charts for international measures corresponding to items you sell (e.g., clothing and cooking utensils). _____

_____

_____

_____

Transportation

List several transportation companies or resources that are able to accommodate special requests. List bilingual transportation/tour resources.

_____

_____

_____

_____

_____

*Several helpful charts and resources are included in Appendix B to assist your international visitors.

Medical, Security, and Identification Issues

Locate critical security information and determine how to make it available in other languages.

_____

_____

_____

List an emergency telephone number that is able to accept emergency or medical phone calls in various languages: _____

_____

_____

_____

Know what types of ID are acceptable for guests who do not hold a U.S. driver's license. _____

_____

_____

_____

Other Issues

Can you think of other resources that your multicultural customers request or need?*

 T h i n k   a b o u t   I t

How Can We Do Better?

In addition to your ideas for improving your own multicultural customer service delivery, you may have recommendations you wish to pass along to others on your team. List up to five recommendations or ideas you have

_____

*Several helpful charts and resources are included in Appendix B to assist your international visitors.

for your co-workers and management team. Identify a strategy for sharing these recommendations with others.

Example: Create a team resource list for serving multicultural customers.

Strategy: Ask team leader to include an "idea exchange" session in a future staff meeting on resources for serving multicultural customers. Use the resource list from this chapter as a starting point.

#1 _____
Strategy: _____
_____
_____

#2 _____
Strategy: _____
_____
_____

#3 _____
Strategy: _____
_____
_____

#4 _____
Strategy: _____
_____
_____

#5 _____
Strategy: _____
_____
_____

5

Chapter 5 Checkpoints

✓ Multicultural customers may have different service expectations and requirements than other customers.

✓ If you want to stand out from your competition, provide a service or product that is sensitive to the needs of your diverse customers.

✓ A four-step process for determining and responding to the needs of multicultural customers is:
- Describe how you typically help a customer.
- Identify typical assumptions you make about customers.
- Check your assumptions to see if they are true for this individual customer.
- Determine how to adapt your customer service to meet the customer's needs.

✓ Plan ahead and put yourself in your customers' shoes to help you anticipate and meet their needs.

✓ Find the balance. Put together a company and community resource team.

6 | Communicating across Cultures

This chapter will help you to:

- Understand how nonverbal communication varies across cultures.
- Recognize cultural differences in verbal communication styles.
- Minimize misunderstandings caused by cultural differences.

Consider the following situations:*

Thomas is a bellman at a vacation ownership resort. His job is to greet customers when they arrive, welcome them to the resort, assist them with their luggage, and direct them to the front desk for check-in. Thomas and the other bellmen are the first employees to interact with a customer when the customer arrives at the resort.

A family from the Middle East has just arrived at the resort. Thomas warmly greets the family, jokes a little with the mother and children, hands the valet ticket to the father, and takes care of the luggage. Then, gesturing with his index finger to "follow me," he escorts the family to the front desk. Upon arriving at the front desk, the parents are visibly upset. The father insists loudly on seeing the manager, to whom he complains about the rude and insolent behavior of the bellman. Thomas is stunned. ■

---

*Comments about these scenarios are found in Appendix A.

■ **T h i n k   a b o u t   I t**

Was Thomas's behavior rude? Why is this customer so upset? How did the family interpret Thomas's behavior? Why? _____

_____

_____

_____

_____

A hotel located in a tourist region books a majority of its room nights for tour and travel groups. Due to the hotel's reservation system, overbookings often occur. When this happens, the front-desk supervisor notifies the tour group upon arrival that they will be transferred to a comparable nearby hotel. Recently the supervisor has recommended to her staff, when possible, to transfer the Japanese tour groups to the other hotel. Americans, she says, get very upset when they are transferred. On the other hand, the Japanese clients don't seem to mind—the hotel hasn't had a single Japanese customer complain about the transfers. ■

What might be happening here from a cultural point of view? How can you learn whether these guests are satisfied or dissatisfied? Why is it important to know? _____

_____

_____

_____

CULTURE'S INFLUENCE ON COMMUNICATION: VERBAL AND NONVERBAL COMMUNICATION

Often, the first thing that comes to mind when we think about multicultural communication is foreign language. Communication, however, is much more than the language we speak. All forms of communication are influenced by culture. Nonverbal language—such as eye contact, body language, facial expressions, and how closely we stand to each other—is directed by our culture. Verbal communication—such as what we speak about, how often we speak, and how we speak—is also influenced by culture.

Because verbal and nonverbal styles of communication change from culture to culture, effectively communicating across cultures can be a little more complex than single culture communications. It requires an understanding of and sensitivity to the power of culture in shaping your communication and that of your multicultural customers.

In this chapter, we will explore how communication varies across culture as introduced in the opening scenarios. In the following chapter, we will look more specifically at communicating with foreign-language customers. We will provide guidelines on making simple adaptations to your verbal and nonverbal communication so that your messages are respectful, meaningful, and effective.

NONVERBAL COMMUNICATION

Nonverbal communication includes all the ways we send and receive information outside of the words we use. Many times we are not aware of the nonverbal communication signals we send. Plus, we may not be aware of the ways we react automatically to others, based on our interpretation of their nonverbal behaviors. Since nonverbal behavior varies from culture to culture, it's important to understand the different meanings it may have for our customers.

Think about It

1. Which of the following nonverbal behaviors have the same meaning universally?
   a. A smile.
   b. Eye contact.

c. The "thumbs-up" sign and "OK" hand gestures.

d. A dozen red roses as a sign of romance.

e. Stepping up very close to someone as a sign of romantic interest (opposite sex) or aggression (same sex).

f. None of the above.

2. How often do people around the world touch each other when
they communicate? On the average, people who know each other
touch each other _____ times per hour?

a. Once or not at all.

b. 2–4 times.

c. 5–10 times.

d. 10–25 times.

e. 25–50 times.

f. 50–100 times.

g. More than 100 times.

h. All of the above.

3. In a meeting or classroom, people should

a. Relax and be comfortable.

b. Sit up straight and remain at attention.

4. People should smell like

a. People.

b. Perfumes, soaps, or cosmetics.

5. When crowds of people are waiting for assistance or to enter an
area, polite behavior includes

a. Standing in line and waiting your turn in first-come, first-serve
fashion, being careful not to touch each other.

b. Moving forward until your find the location that you desire. It's
OK to make physical contact with others.

6. When there is a long silence in a conversation, it usually feels

a. Awkward or uncomfortable. Someone will usually try to think
of something to say.

b. Comfortable. Silence shows respect for the speaker or the
speaker's words, or shows that the listeners feel the topic is
important.

NONVERBAL BEHAVIOR IN CONTEXT

As you can see from this quiz, there are many issues to consider when looking at nonverbal behavior from a multicultural perspective. In the guidelines that follow, take note of how closely nonverbal behavior is tied into cultural context.

In item one, the focus is on the cultural connotation of a smile. The smile is one of the few gestures that is understood universally. It represents a sign of goodwill. There are cultural differences, however, in how often we smile, at whom we smile, and the many additional meanings that a smile can have. Paired with other nonverbals—such as eye contact, tilt of the head, body stance, and tone of voice— smiles can also convey messages related to aggression, anger, nervousness, and sexuality.

The other nonverbal behaviors—eye contact, hand gestures, color, symbols (such as the meaning of flowers), and how closely we stand—all vary significantly by culture. For example, in Native American, many Asian, and some Hispanic cultures, looking down and avoiding direct eye contact is a sign of respect. The "thumbs-up" sign, a favorite gesture in the United States, is an obscene gesture in Iran and Spain. The "OK" gesture means "worthless" or "zero" in France and is obscene or impolite in Greece, parts of Eastern Europe, and Latin America. If the gesture is made with the hand pointed down at the floor, it is the sign of money in Japan. In the United Kingdom, the "victory" sign is made with palm in. Palm out V signs (used for "victory" or "peace" in the United States) mean "up yours" in Great Britain.

The meanings of colors and flowers differ around the world. In China, blue and white are colors of mourning. Purple flowers mean death in Brazil. Flowers of mourning are chrysanthemums in France and carnations in Germany. In many Western European countries, flowers are presented in odd numbers because presenting an even number of flowers brings bad luck.

6

There is tremendous variation around the world in use of personal space. For example, in the Middle East, people of the same sex stand much closer together than do Americans. It is not uncommon for men to stand within a foot of each other during discussion, while people of the opposite sex stand much further apart than do Americans. In Japan, two Japanese men may stand four to five feet apart when talking, except on crowded transportation vehicles.

In item two, all answers are correct. Mainstream Americans tend to touch between two and four times per hour. People from the U.K. and parts of northern Europe and Asia touch much less. In France, Italy, and many Hispanic countries, people tend to touch much more frequently. In some cultures, very close friends can be observed touching each other more than 100 times per hour. Actual touching "rules" vary widely by country, culture, gender, and social hierarchy.

Posture, the focus in item three, differs around the world. In the United States, casual posture and dress are appreciated. Elsewhere posture is often more erect, which demonstrates attention and respect.

For some Americans, smell is one of the most powerful nonverbal communicators. The human body should smell of soaps, perfumes, or cosmetics, but never body odor. Any individual who "smells bad" is easily dismissed as undesirable. Many other cultural groups are comfortable with body smells and do not understand this American cultural norm.

Audience and group behavior among cultural groups vary widely as shown in item five. For example, standing in line is culturally learned behavior. Alternative methods include jostling to establish position and allowing group hierarchy to determine who goes first. Other aspects of public space vary as well. For example, in Singapore, upon boarding a bus, if only one passenger is on the bus, it's polite to sit down in the seat next to that person. In the United States, this would be a sign of aggression; an individual would be careful to leave extra seats between himself and the other passenger.

Item six brings up the issue of silence. Many Americans will try to fill silence in conversations, as silence is a sign of discomfort or awkwardness. In other parts of the world, such as in much of Asia, silence is appreciated and can be a sign of importance or respect.

All of these examples show how nonverbal behavior can vary from culture to culture. Nonverbal communication includes touch, smell, taste, color, personal and public space, symbols, silence, facial expressions, posture, gestures and other body language, gift giving, and use of time.

WHY IS NONVERBAL COMMUNICATION SO IMPORTANT?

Understanding nonverbal communication is important because:

- Seventy to ninety-three percent or more of all communication is nonverbal. The rest of communication is verbal.
- We often make powerful, instantaneous, subconscious judgments about people based on their nonverbal behavior.
- Nonverbal behavior varies by culture. Facial expression, hand gesture, or body posture can mean different things in different cultures.
- The more diverse our customer base is, the more likely we are to come into contact with nonverbal behavior different than our own.
- If we interpret the nonverbal behavior of one culture based on the meaning that behavior has in another culture, we are very often mistaken.

Think about It

Although we seldom stop to think about nonverbal behavior, we have very strong emotional responses to it. The following exercises will demonstrate the power of nonverbal behavior. While talking with a friend or colleague:

- Stand five inches closer to the person than you normally would.
- Reach out and touch your friend or colleague on the arm several times more than you normally would during a conversation.
- Avoid making eye contact for at least two or three minutes.

After completing this activity, explain to your friend or colleague that you are investigating reactions to nonverbal behavior. What are your feelings and your colleague's reactions to these changes in behavior?

TIPS FOR MORE EFFECTIVE NONVERBAL COMMUNICATION ACROSS CULTURES

1. Let your customers use nonverbal communication that is most comfortable for them. For example, if a customer stands closer to you than you normally prefer, try not to back up. If the customer moves away from you, try not to inch forward to make yourself more comfortable. This takes a conscious effort; we are often unaware of our reactions to nonverbal behavior.

2. Adapt your nonverbal behavior; don't mimic your customer. A common mistake is to try to mirror the customers' nonverbal behavior in an attempt to adapt to her style. This can backfire. A better guideline is to simply tone down your nonverbal communication if it is more animated than your customer's. For example, if you use large, sweeping gestures and your customer uses no gestures, you may wish to be more reserved with your gestures. Or if you like to shake hands, yet your customer seems uncomfortable doing so, don't force the customer to shake your hand. But if your customer is more animated than you, do not exaggerate your style to match the customer's style; this often comes off as mocking or insincere.

3. Avoid gestures and body language that are offensive. Some examples of nonverbal American behavior that can be offensive in different cultures include the OK sign, the peace or victory gesture, keeping the hands in the pockets, standing with your hands on your hips, slouching in a chair, putting your feet up on furniture, showing the soles of the feet, touching someone's head, touching with the left hand, gesturing with the index finger, or slapping your fist in your palm. It's very simple to avoid using these and other possibly offensive gestures that you learn about.

4. Stop and think. Occasionally a multicultural customer may react unexpectedly to you or may do something you find offensive. Before jumping to conclusions about the customer, stop and ask yourself if there is a possible cultural explanation. For instance, a customer who avoids making eye contact with you may lead you to think that he is shy or perhaps even dishonest and hiding something. Knowing that eye contact varies by culture, and that in some cultures averting your gaze is a way to demonstrate respect, you will be more likely to interpret this behavior correctly.

VERBAL COMMUNICATION STYLES

6

Like nonverbal communication, verbal communication varies by culture. Americans have developed a communication style that favors direct, simple, efficient communication. We tend to value getting to the point and giving our opinion even if it is different than someone else's. Although we voice differences of opinion, we try to do so in a way that avoids argument or debate.

These cultural "rules" are not expressly taught in books. We learn these lessons as children from our parents and teachers. We reinforce them in the workplace, in the media, and in our personal relationships. And then we teach them to our children. Over the course of a lifetime, we learn:

- What is OK to talk about and what is taboo to talk about.
- How much we should say or should not say.
- How we should greet each other.
- With whom we should speak.
- How to express agreement and disagreement in acceptable ways.

How many of the following proverbs and teachings have you heard? Fill in the blank with the very first thought that comes to mind. Then compare your phrases with those suggested below.

Don't beat around the _____.   Stick to the _____.
If it's important, speak _____.
He was talking out of both sides _____.
I heard it straight from the _____.

Common responses: Don't beat around the bush. / Stick to the point. Stick to the subject. / If it's important, say so. If it's important, speak up. / He was talking out of both sides of his mouth. / I heard it straight from the horse's mouth.

These proverbs are not universal. If you had grown up in another part of the world, you would have heard very different lessons about communication.

6

TEN WAYS THAT COMMUNICATION STYLES VARY ACROSS CULTURES

Following are 10 pairs of sentences that show how "good" communication differs across cultures.

Task orientation. It's important to take care of business without wasting excessive time on small talk and getting to know each other.

Relationship orientation. Building relationships is more important than completing tasks. People cannot do business together until they have taken time to establish a relationship.

Clarity. It is best to be clear and specific in expressing and requesting information. Beating around the bush is annoying or a sign that people are evading the truth.

Complexity. It is best to be vague and ambiguous when expressing information. Speaking in a direct, straightforward way is unnecessarily harsh and impolite.

Face-to-face communication. Two people should work out their problems directly with each other.

Use of third party. The best way to work out problems between two people is to use an intermediary or go-between.

Emphasis on words. If something is important or on your mind, you should speak up.

Emphasis on context. If something is important, it should be left unsaid. Putting everything into words weakens communication and relationships.

Importance of individual opinion. People should express their individual points of view and opinions even if they differ from the beliefs or opinions held by others in the group.

Importance of harmony. Disagreeing with others, pointing out mistakes, or insisting on personal opinions can undermine a group. It causes group disharmony and loss of face.

Supportive discussion. When disagreeing with or criticizing others, it's important to do so in a positive, supportive manner. A person may feel personally attacked when someone else argues with her.

Critical discussion. Arguing, debating, and criticizing ideas are enjoyable and acceptable conversational styles. One should point out the weakness in the other person's argument as this promotes the exchange of ideas.

Expression of emotion. It is OK to share feelings such as happiness, excitement, enthusiasm, or sadness through words or facial expressions.

Suppression of emotion. It is important and thoughtful to hide all personal feelings and opinions so that they are not evident in words or facial expressions.

Detached/objective style. In meetings, people should stay rational and in control of their emotions. Becoming overly emotional takes away from the speaker's credibility and effectiveness.

Animated style. Becoming louder and animated is a sign of involvement in the discussion. A person who remains unanimated during the discussion may be insincere or not interested in the topic.

Simplicity. It's best to simplify ideas, clarify thoughts, and avoid ambiguity.

Complexity. Simplicity should be distrusted. Complex communication reflects the depth of the topic.

Concrete. The best way to learn or to solve a problem is to examine and discuss concrete examples.

Theoretical. The best way to learn or to solve a problem is to discuss the underlying theory and philosophy.

DIFFERENT DOES NOT MEAN DEFICIENT

As you read through the previous descriptions of different communication styles, did you find yourself more comfortable with the statements on the left or on the right? The phrases on the left describe the American "mainstream" or most widely used communication style, although many variations exist. The phrases on the right represent alternative communication styles that are found in various cultural groups, both in the United States and abroad. For example, almost all cultures in the world place more emphasis on relationship building than do the majority of Americans. Asian cultures tend to value harmony and may suppress personal feelings or opinions in order to promote group cohesiveness and harmony. Middle Eastern and some European and African-American cultures tend to value a more intense, animated, personal, argumentative conversational style than is typically found in Anglo-American culture.

The first reaction many people have when they encounter someone with an unfamiliar communication style is to wonder why the other person communicates "like that." It's fairly common to feel that your own style is "right," "natural," or "normal." You might say, *"Why was he so rude?" "Why didn't she speak up?" "If she was dissatisfied, she should have told me." "He said yes and nodded his head, and now I find out he didn't mean yes at all."* In reality, our way of communicating strikes many people from other cultures as oddly as their style strikes us.

6

When two people are using the same communication "rules," there is a pretty good chance they will understand each other. When two people from different cultures communicate, they may unknowingly be playing by different communication rules. In this case, communication breaks down more easily. Knowing about differences, accepting and respecting differences, and communicating in a way that is comfortable for both you *and* your multicultural customer, are the keys to minimizing cultural misunderstanding.

BICULTURAL COMMUNICATION SKILLS

Many Americans have been influenced by multiple cultural groups. For example, a first-generation Asian-American child may utilize a communication style at home that is subtle, indirect, and respectful of family harmony and hierarchy. This reflects the Asian communication style, although variations exist between countries and between individuals. At school, the child may interact with teachers and classmates in the mainstream American communication style that is more direct, informal, and specific. Many other examples exist. For instance, a Native American may communicate in his traditional style at home, but may adopt a mainstream style at school or at work. Men and women often have differences in communication styles as well.

Individuals who are exposed to several cultures may be comfortable with and fluent in various cultural communication styles. These people are "bicultural" or "multicultural."

Those of us who have never been exposed to another culture, or who are in the midst of adapting to a new culture ourselves, can acquire multicultural skills through reading, learning about others, and practicing. We can also ask bicultural colleagues to assist us with our multicultural customers. However, it's important to remember that not every individual who looks, sounds, or seems bicultural to you is willing and able to serve as a cultural interpreter. It's important to ask them first about their experience, comfort level, and interest in the culture you are learning about.

TIPS FOR EFFECTIVE CROSS-CULTURAL COMMUNICATION

6

Allow your customer to set the pace, tone, and style.   If your customer wants to spend extra time getting to know you, try to allot the time. It is time well spent. If your customer chooses to communicate through an intermediary, don't blame the customer for not speaking to you directly. If their style is formal, enjoy it. Formality denotes respect in many cultures. There are numerous cues your customers will give you about their communication styles.

Adapt your communication style.   You are already experienced in adapting your communication style—you act differently at a ball game or in church, with your family or with strangers, with your company president or with your closest co-worker. Use this skill to make slight adaptations to your own behavior when serving multicultural customers. One simple adaptation is to always err on the side of respectful communication.

Don't assume that yes means yes.   Many customers will say yes to avoid embarrassment. They may not wish to embarrass themselves or you by disagreeing with you or indicating they can't understand you. This could cause you or them to lose face.

Avoid saying no.   Many Americans answer questions with the simple word *no*. This very direct (and negative) communication style is jarring to many customers. For multicultural customers, it may seem even more harsh. While you may not be able to accommodate every customer's request, you can present the information in a respectful way that is less abrupt. Adding an apology, along with solutions to the customer's requests, is helpful.

Get comfortable with ambiguity.   Cross-cultural communication is complex and uncertain. You may not always understand everything that is happening and that's OK. You can be effective even if you don't fully understand a culture.

Enjoy rather than judge.   You will encounter many differences in the ways customers communicate. Enjoy the differences rather than become annoyed by them. You will expand your perspective and meet interesting new people.

6

Chapter 6 Checkpoints

✓ Culture has a powerful influence on your communication, both verbal and nonverbal.

✓ Expectations that others will conform to your rules of verbal and nonverbal communication can lead to breakdowns in communication.

✓ Knowing about cultural differences does not give you the "right" answer about what different behaviors mean. Cultural knowledge does give you *additional* information to consider in analyzing behavior.

✓ Take your cue from your customers. They will communicate, verbally and nonverbally, in ways that are comfortable for them.

✓ Adapt your communication and behavior, where appropriate, to make your customers more comfortable.

✓ Don't abandon your own culture. Generally, the most comfortable multicultural solution is to find a midpoint that reflects your own culture and demonstrates respect for the culture of your customer.

7 | Communicating across Language Differences

This chapter will help you to:

- Improve your communication across language barriers.
- Increase your listening skills across language barriers.
- Provide better customer service for customers with limited or no English skills.
- Reduce the stress that is often associated with language differences.

Consider the following situation:*

Gerald is a customer representative for a large information services firm. He receives a phone call from a customer with a foreign accent. Upon hearing the accent, Gerald loudly asks the customer to hold and transfers the call to a bilingual co-worker. ■

■ Think about It

Is this good customer service? What could Gerald do differently in the future to ensure that he is providing outstanding customer service for foreign-language or multilingual customers? _____

_____

_____

———————————
*Comments about this scenario are found in Appendix A.

There are many different terms that describe individuals who are speaking a foreign language. Common terminology used to describe an individual for whom English is a foreign language includes *non-native speaker of English, limited-English language speaker, foreign speaker of English, and speaker of English as a second language.* Other terms you may hear include *bilingual* for a person who speaks two languages and *multilingual* for a person who speaks two or more languages. The terms are used interchangeably in this chapter; our focus is on you, the customer service provider, and any customer who experiences language difficulties while interacting with you.

MEETING THE NEEDS OF THE MULTILINGUAL CUSTOMER

Overcoming language barriers is an important part of providing multicultural customer service. In the United States alone there are nearly 150 languages spoken. And millions of travelers to the United States each year are from countries where English is not the primary language. Plus, in some English-speaking countries (consider Australia and the United Kingdom), the language is quite different than American English.

Even if you and your customer do not speak the same language, you can still provide outstanding customer service. In Chapter 5 you identified language resources for helping foreign-language customers. This chapter focuses on how you can adapt *your own* manner of speaking and listening. By doing so, you and your multilingual customers will be better able to understand each other. This chapter will also help you to avoid the common pitfalls encountered when attempting to serve customers with language differences. As a result, you will enhance the quality of your customer service and reduce stress for both you and your customer.

Interaction Is the Key

Outstanding customer service is a personal interaction. It takes place between you and your customer, often one customer at a time. Take a moment to think about your current and potential customers and answer the following questions about language and your customers:

- What languages do I speak or understand?
- What percentage of my current or potential customers speak a language other than English as their primary language?
- What languages do my customers speak or understand?
- What language difficulties do my customers experience when communicating with me or my co-workers?
- What am I currently doing to enhance my ability to communicate across language barriers?
- What am I currently doing that undermines my ability to communicate across language barriers?

SPEAKING EFFECTIVELY ACROSS LANGUAGE BARRIERS

Often when speaking to customers who do not speak English as their native language, we speak to them as if they had full command of our language or as if they had no understanding at all. In reality, many customers are somewhere in between. By making some simple adaptations to your word choice and pacing, you will greatly enhance your chances of being understood by a person with limited English skills.

Four Tips on Word Choice

Practice adapting your speaking by restating each sentence to make it easier to understand. Then compare your answers with those suggested.

1. Use words that are simple, common English.
"There are multiple perspectives that must be taken into consideration when reviewing this problem." _____

_____

2. Choose the most simple, direct, grammatical form possible.
"Would you be so kind as to repeat what you just said; I'm not quite sure I understood." _____

3. Avoid jargon, slang, idiomatic expressions, and acronyms. *
"We thought we had all the wrinkles ironed out, but we hit a snafu."

_____

"I'm not sure I can handle that for you. Perhaps you'll want to talk with the CSR." _____

4. Use direct language rather than passive language.
"The form must be filled out in its entirety with no questions omitted."

_____

Possible answers:

"There are several ideas to consider regarding this problem."

"I do not understand. Please repeat." (or) "I'm sorry. What did you say?"

"We thought we had done/completed/solved everything. But then we found a problem."

"The customer service representative can help you with this."

"Please answer every question on the form."

Five Tips on Pacing

Another way that you can modify your speech to make it easier to understand is to change its speed and the flow of thoughts.

1. Organize your thoughts. Before you begin to speak, arrange the contents of your message in a clear, concise way. Decide what the most important point is and focus on the essential information. Try to avoid information overload.

_____

Jargon is special scientific or technical vocabulary words used within a particular subject matter. *Slang* is informal language used by a group of people. An *idiomatic expression* is a group of words that, together, have a special meaning that has nothing to do with the meaning of each word in the expression (e.g., "It's raining cats and dogs."). An *acronym* is an abbreviation used as a word (e.g., TV for *television*).

2. Break messages down into manageable pieces. Use short sentences. Complete a thought before moving on to the next item. Meandering, run-on sentences, so common in American speech, can be hard to follow for speakers with limited English skills. (This sentence is an example.)

3. Speak slowly. The average American speaks at a rate of 300 syllables per minute. While many of us know that speaking more slowly helps a listener with limited English abilities, few people actually make this simple change. It takes practice to speak more slowly, but it's worth the effort. Remember that if you are going to speak more slowly, you will need to schedule more time for the conversation. A simple guideline is to allot twice as much time for communication across language barriers as you would allot for conversations with same-language speakers.

4. Enunciate each word. In normal speech, many sounds or complete syllables are run together or omitted. For example, *"What do you want to do today?"* may be pronounced *"Whaduhyu wanna do duday?"* Pronouncing words carefully will help your listener to understand what you are saying. Using this same phrase *"What do you want to do today?"* pronounce it aloud as you would normally. Then restate it, enunciating each word. Notice the difference in how you sound and the additional time it takes to enunciate clearly.

5. Allow pauses between sentences or after questions. Compared with various other cultural groups, many Americans tend to be uncomfortable with silence. When there is a pause in the conversation, we will often jump in to clarify what has just been said. For example, you'll often hear, "What I mean is . . ." and then the sentence will be restated or elaborated. For a limited-English speaker, this is confusing. Allow pauses. They provide time for mental translation.

Think about It

Using the word choice and pacing tips, restate the following paragraphs so that they will be easier to understand for someone with limited English-language skills. Ask a friend or colleague to provide feedback on your word choice and pacing. (Or you may wish to record this exercise on a tape recorder and evaluate your own abilities.)

"We were brainstorming the other day and an idea hit me. Right off the bat I knew it would be a winner. Here, let me run it by you and see how it strikes you." _____

_____

_____

_____

"As we've discussed, I've met with my management and we have concluded that at this time it is not possible for our store to provide you a refund or to replace your damaged merchandise in light of the fact that you have worn the item several times and have laundered it in a way that is inconsistent with the instructions provided on the label. We do value your patronage and hope to have the opportunity to serve you again in the future, but we do ask that you return any item with which you are not satisfied more promptly so that we may assist you to your complete satisfaction." _____

_____

_____

_____

LISTENING ACROSS LANGUAGE DIFFERENCES

Listening skills are just as important as speaking skills when it comes to communicating effectively across language differences.

Rate yourself in the following skills and characteristics for effective listening across language differences.

	Almost Always	Sometimes	Almost Never
1. I am willing to spend extra energy to listen to others who have language difficulties.	_____	_____	_____
2. I am able to focus on the message rather than the accent or language errors.	_____	_____	_____
3. I am patient. I allot/give sufficient time and do not rush or interrupt the limited-English speaker.	_____	_____	_____
4. I recognize my own personal pet peeves regarding language and I do not let the pet peeves stop me from listening.	_____	_____	_____
5. I do not judge the worth of the other person or the content of the message simply on the speaker's English proficiency level or communication style.	_____	_____	_____
6. I ask questions to clarify and confirm understanding.	_____	_____	_____
7. I know the common pitfalls for foreign speakers of English and I do not get confused when the speaker chooses the wrong word or grammatical structure.	_____	_____	_____
8. I avoid getting frustrated.	_____	_____	_____
9. I avoid using "he doesn't speak English well" as an excuse for lack of respect or concern about a person's needs.	_____	_____	_____

7

UNDERSTANDING COMMON LANGUAGE DIFFICULTIES

Foreign-speakers of any language are likely to make mistakes when speaking the language. Common mistakes include:

- Choosing the wrong words.
- Using the wrong word endings.

- Confusing pronouns (e.g. he/she, his/her).
- Mispronouncing words.
- Stressing the wrong words or syllables.
- Speaking in a pitch or rhythm that sounds unusual.

These common language difficulties, combined with the nonverbal and communication style differences discussed in the previous chapter, add to the complexity of your interaction with multicultural customers. A successful listener across language differences is able to pick out the correct message in spite of errors and accents. Once you become comfortable with common language errors, and if you practice listening intently to foreign speakers of English, you will increase your ability to understand across language barriers. Here are some examples of the common language errors you will hear.

Mispronounced Words

Foreign speakers of English use the sounds they learned in their own language as they attempt to speak English. But many sounds in English don't exist in other languages, so certain English sounds will consistently be mispronounced. For example, Japanese speakers often struggle with the American *r* and *l* sounds, while Spanish speakers have difficulty with *sh* and *ch* sounds and words starting in *s*. French speakers may not say the English *h* sound at all or may have difficulty with *th* sounds.

Skill: A skilled listener will recognize common errors made by foreign speakers and will not be sidetracked from listening and understanding.

"Polite" Language

In any language, there are ways to make statements more "polite." Foreign speakers of English often haven't mastered these advanced language skills. As a result, they may sound rude, pushy, or immature. For instance, look at the sentences below. All have the same meaning, but each one is more grammatically complex and more "polite." The foreign speaker of English will often know only the simple, most direct forms.

Coffee. ⇨ *I want coffee.* ⇨ *I would like coffee.* ⇨ *I would like some coffee.* ⇨ *May I have some coffee?*

Skill: The careful listener will not make automatic decisions about politeness, rudeness, or intelligence based on a foreign speaker's use of simple statements.

Intonation

Learning the intonation or inflection of a language is difficult. So, even if the words are correct, the rise and fall of the voice can be confusing. Two examples follow:

- A foreign speaker of English raises her voice at the end of each statement, as is customary in her own language. The American listener incorrectly assumes she is asking a question or is unsure of herself.
- A person speaks with a high-pitched voice, which is correct for the native language. It is irritating to the American listener as the speaker sounds harsh or like she is complaining.

These and other differences in tone or voice inflection can be misleading to the unskilled listener.

Read the following sentences aloud, stressing a different word each time.

I will discuss it with you later.

I **will** discuss it with you later.

I will **discuss** it with you later.

I will discuss it with **you** later.

I will discuss it with you **later**.

Say the following sentence aloud, stressing the syllables that are marked in bold.

He no**rmal**ly stress**ed** the se**cond** sy**lla**ble.

You can see how difficult these simple sentences are to understand correctly when the speaker makes a few simple intonation "mistakes."

Skill: The skilled listener recognizes intonation mistakes and avoids judging the speaker based on intonation.

FOUR TIPS ON SPEAKING YOUR CUSTOMER'S LANGUAGE

The focus of this chapter has been to help you adapt your own speaking and listening habits to communicate more clearly with customers who have limited abilities in your language. There are also times when it's important for you to speak their language. Here are a few tips to assist you.

1. Learn some of the language. Whenever possible, learn a few phrases in your customers' languages. Greetings, thank you, and a few of the common phrases you use every day go a long way in letting your customers know you are interested in them. Even the smallest language efforts on your part help customers release stress, and will help you build trust and bring warmth to the interaction. And, of course, if you learn more of the language, so much the better.

2. Provide written materials. Try to provide important information in writing. The customer can then read the materials at his own pace, stopping to figure out difficult words. One helpful guideline is to always write down numbers, which are difficult to comprehend and remember in a foreign language.

If you have many customers who speak the same language, have important information translated into that language by a professional translator. Translations of product and safety information, required forms, location guidebooks, and other frequently used materials will help both you and the customer.

3. Utilize interpreters. Sometimes the best way to help customers is to serve them in their own language. Interpreters will assist you in doing this. If you are already helping a customer, and you would like to bring in an interpreter, ask permission first. Many customers, regardless of accent or difficulty in English, enjoy speaking the language and prefer not to have an interpreter. They may be insulted if you pass them off to an interpreter automatically. On the other hand, if the customer would like an interpreter and one is available, utilizing an interpreter is one way to provide outstanding customer service.

4. Choose interpreters carefully. When utilizing interpreters, it's always best to use trained professionals. As this is not always possible, another option is to identify, in advance, bilingual co-workers or contacts who are willing to assist you with foreign-language customers. Choose your interpreters carefully. A common mistake is to believe that any bilingual person can serve as an interpreter. This is not true and leads to many unfortunate interpretation disasters. Choose interpreters who are willing and experienced and who have proven interpretation abilities.

SOME ADDITIONAL DO'S AND DON'T'S

Do ...

Be patient.   It takes extra effort and time to communicate across language barriers. However, the increase in your customer service capabilities makes it well worth the effort.

Use visual support.   When possible, provide charts and brief, clearly written materials.

Check for understanding.   It is helpful to repeat or rephrase your customer's request to be sure you understand correctly.

Enjoy yourself.   Many of your customers will appreciate your special efforts to communicate with them. You can gain great satisfaction and enjoyment from working with different-language customers!

Don't . . .

Yell or raise your voice.   Unfortunately, this is a common mistake that many well-intentioned customer service providers make.

Condescend.   Speakers with accents are not stupid or uneducated. A foreign accent tells you only that the person speaks more than one language.

Complete their sentences.   Bite your tongue, if you must, but try not to interrupt.

Criticize or laugh.   Don't belittle their English or blame them for their difficulty in communication.

7

Chapter 7 Checkpoints

✓ Effective communicators across language differences take responsibility for the success of the communication rather than blame the other person's lack of language ability.

✓ By adapting the way you speak and listen, you will be better able to communicate with and serve limited-English-language customers.

✓ The more you listen to your foreign-language customers, the more you will understand their particular ways of speaking English.

✓ Each customer is different. Some may want to utilize English while others greatly appreciate translation or interpretation. Take the customers' feelings and desires into account as you choose how best to help them.

✓ Try to learn a few phrases in your customers' languages.

8 | Multicultural Customer Service: Service Examples and Heroes

This chapter will help you to:

- Gain examples of organizations and service representatives who have improved their level of customer service for their muticultural customers.
- Include new ideas for serving multicultural customers in your job.
- Make a commitment for providing quality service to your multicultural customers.

Throughout this book we have discussed situations in which multicultural customers (1) need products or services outside of the requests that you commonly hear or (2) ask that their needs be met in ways that have value and meaning to them. In this chapter you will read about people just like you who are making a difference. You will also be introduced to various organizational systems designed to help customer service representatives meet the needs of their multicultural customers.

In many cases you will notice that the organization or service provider has made simple adaptations in their product or in the way they deliver that product to their customers. As a result they have improved the level of customer service provided to all of their customers. This is certainly not an exhaustive list—there are many more examples of good multicultural customer service in countless organizations around the United States.

Through sharing these examples, our goal is to inspire you to look at and try a variety of ways to provide quality service to all your customers:

the ones who speak your language and share similar customs and those who don't.

GOVERNMENT

The City of Tulsa, Oklahoma

"In a city, we must deliver services to everyone. Citizens are our customers, and delivering service the best way possible is key! Citizens are the best observers of how we do what we do," says Jeannie McDaniels of the mayor's office. Like many other cities throughout the United States, Tulsa is experiencing an increase in its diverse population. The greatest growth has occurred in the Hispanic community, which has increased over 50 percent in the Tulsa metropolitan area. The Tulsa Police Department wanted to be responsive to situations involving Hispanics who may or may not speak English.

Here's what the city of Tulsa is doing:

- An eight-hour block of training was developed that included "street survival" Spanish (words and phrases appropriate to law enforcement needs) as well as a session on cultural aspects of the Spanish community.

- The Spanish-Speaking Ride-Along Program allows members of the Hispanic community, who meet certain criteria as judged by the Hispanic Affairs Commission, to ride with a police officer during her shift. Two initial benefits are derived: (1) it provides an immediate interpreter if an officer encounters a language barrier and (2) it provides an opportunity for the officer to practice her newly acquired Spanish skills.

- The department identified a 30-week extended language training course for officers as a next step in their skill development.

The city believes that these initiatives have sensitized the department to the needs of ethnic groups and illustrated the benefits of working together to meet the needs of various community groups.

What can you do?   How can you begin to acquire some "survival" language skills including some of the basic words and phrases of your multicultural customers?

Action Steps:_____

_____

EDUCATION
University of Houston
Houston, Texas

In 1994, the University of Houston ranked 15th among universities that serve international students. A full 110 foreign countries (about 2,200 students—about 7 percent of the student population) are represented at the university. Dr. Adria Baker of the Office of International Admissions believes this is a win–win situation for the university, the students, and the countries to which these students will return. "These students add flavor to our discussions by offering international perspectives, they increase the diversity within the University, and they make our programs stronger and more prestigious." The Office of International Admissions works to take care of students during the application process by helping international students and families feel more comfortable. By gaining a better understanding of their educational system and then helping them understand ours, the customer service is better and the process is smoother.

Here are a few examples:

- The university offers an Arrival Booklet for international students as well as an International Student Handbook which gives tips on housing arrangements, payment methods, initial cash requirements, dealing with U.S. banks, arrival instructions, and special airport pickup services offered by community volunteers.

- All correspondence to potential international students is customized so that the students and their families can better understand

and fulfill university admission requirements. For example, for U.S. students the form might read, "Please send a copy of your transcripts." The customized form might read, "Please submit proof of your degree conferred." Other wording differences include India, Pakistan, and Bangladesh's *marksheets* for our word *credentials* and Canada's *calendar* for our word *catalog*. Another interesting tip to keep in mind when asking for someone's date of birth is to specify date of birth according to the western calendar.

Overall, Dr. Baker has learned that students from some cultures vary in the degree of formality they prefer, but most students prefer a more personal touch. However, customer service is always important.

What can you do?   How can you adapt the way you speak and listen so that you can better communicate across cultures? How can you recognize when you have used a common English word that may be misunderstood in other cultures?

Action Steps: _____

_____

8

TELECOMMUNICATIONS
AT&T
New Jersey

One of the most common needs of any traveler is to use the telephone to reach home or the office. As telephone systems vary around the world, this simple task can be confusing for international callers. Unfortunately, when international visitors ask for telephone information, the employee at the front desk, the guest service counter, or the information center is often unaware of international calling procedures. Hotels or other service providers can often team with their telecommunications company to better service the customer. AT&T services that assist international callers include bilingual information call guides and emergency translation services.

Here's an example:

- AT&T provides country-specific calling information cards that may be displayed in hotel lobbies. They explain the easiest, fastest way to call a customer's home country from a hotel room.
- Language Line and Interpretation Assistance covers 140 languages.
- International Fax Service provides support staff to assist with international faxing.
- International 800 Service helps friends and customers in other countries call a company more conveniently.
- Pamphlets discuss the do's and don't's of international trade.

Here are samples of country-specific calling information cards, in this case for Mexico and Israel.

8

What can you do?   In addition to knowing how to complete international calls, it also helps to keep a time zone chart available to answer
questions about time differences so that you can place your international
calls at the appropriate time. Many customer service providers learn this
the hard way by unknowingly phoning their customers in the middle of
the night.

Action Steps:_____
_____

Sprint
Kansas City, Kansas

Sprint is a diversified international telecommunications company providing global voice, video, and data communications services and related products. The long-distance division serves nearly 8 million customers with the only nationwide 100 percent digital, fiberoptic network in the United States. It also provides voice services to more than 290 countries and locations.

In an effort to understand the problems and concerns of multinational customers in the United States, Sprint commissioned a survey to measure the degree of confusion newcomers to the United States may have adjusting to the telephone services available to them. Areas of concern were understanding the phone bill, dialing 411 for a local number, understanding the White and Yellow Pages in a telephone book, and using 911.

Here's what Sprint is doing:

- As a result of this study, Sprint and the U.S. Office of Consumer Affairs hired a consumer group to run public service announcements about the U.S. phone system in Spanish and English.
- Plans are underway to distribute educational material in English, Chinese, Korean, and Spanish.
- Customers have access to in-language operator assistance 24 hours a day, seven days a week for help with international calling.
- Operators are available who speak Cantonese, English, French, German, Japanese, Mandarin, Polish, Russian, Spanish, and Tagalog (the language of the Philippines).

What can you do?   What difficulties may your multicultural customers have that you may have never considered?

Action Steps:_____

8

HEALTHCARE

The Methodist Hospital
Houston, Texas

The internationally renowned Methodist Hospital has about 6 percent of its 100,000 plus patients come from 88 countries annually. The hospital provides complete red-carpet service. The Methodist Hospital has always attracted and received international patients due to its high-quality medical and nursing staff, its technological and research advances, and its excellent services. In the 1980s, a formal department was formed to assist patients when they arrived. Now there are two different international areas: (1)The International Affairs Department, which handles physician-to-physician and hospital-to-hospital relationships and marketing activities with other countries; and (2) The International Patient Services Department, which assists patients before and during their visit to the hospital and after they return to their country. As Patricia Chalupsky, RN and Manager of International Patient Services explains, "once international patients interact with us, they see and feel the difference in the way we deliver service. We want to relieve their anxieties, make them feel as comfortable as possible and fulfill their needs in the most immediate and culturally sensitive manner."

Here are some examples:

- The hospital contacts the patients before they leave their country to provide information, answer questions, and preadmit the patient. Preadmission is very helpful so that when a tired, ill person who has traveled many miles arrives at the hospital, he or she can go directly to a room to rest and begin their medical assessment and treatment plan.

- The Airport Patient Facilitation Program is a collaborative effort between the hospital, the Department of Aviation, and the City of Houston. A City of Houston representative, who speaks the patient's language, meets and greets patients and their families when they deplane. There is a wheelchair, ambulance, helicopter, or other ground transportation ready. The patients are given a welcome card with a 24-hour phone number and a person to contact at any point during their stay.

- This culturally informed representative assists the patients and their families with their luggage and escorts them to U.S. Customs and Immigration Services for more immediate processing.

- Once in the hospital, a multilingual, multicultural hospital International Patient Representative meets them and delivers a welcome letter in the patient's language, informing them of the various services delivered by the International Patient Services Department and the hospital.

- The hospital's Dietary Services will prepare meals that fit the patient's dietary needs and ethnic desires.

- The Serving the World Volunteer Program is staffed by hospital employees and community volunteers who are bilingual and culturally sensitive. These volunteers visit the patient and accompanying members and offer an understanding and supportive relationship.

- Reading materials, such as newspapers and magazines, as well as television programming, movies and cassette tapes are available in different languages.

- A designated Muslim prayer room is provided for those of the Islamic faith. If requested, a compass is provided to assist Muslim patients to determine East for prayer. A prayer rug, a *Koran,* and religious tapes are also available. Other religious services are provided for other faiths, and services in Spanish are also conducted.

- The department also assists the patient to meet governmental regulations, get visa extension, and write letters to employers and to airlines to change flight schedules and tickets so that they will not be unduly penalized due to the necessary healthcare stay.

- Inservices and presentations are provided to hospital staff to increase cultural awareness and sensitivity, thereby promoting a blend of various cultures to deliver the best services possible.

What can you do?   Anticipating and meeting the needs of your customers and delivering the services to them in a culturally sensitive way is an important part of customer service. How can you plan ahead so that you are ready with information, products, and services that may be helpful to the particular population you are serving?

Action Steps:_____

_____

BANKING

First Interstate Bank
Los Angeles, California

With 1,167 offices in 13 western states, First Interstate Bankcorp is the 14th largest bank in the United States. Leslie Weigle, Training Research Development, explains that the First Interstate's mission is to "provide superior value and exceptional service to all customers ... By valuing the diversity of our clients, employees, vendors, and communities in which we work, we stand to deliver the best service possible and to establish long-term, loyal, and profitable relationships in every aspect of our business."

Here are some examples:

- Richard Wyler, vice president and media relations officer, reported that First Interstate recently set out to address the needs of its Chinese-American customers in California. Because the Chinese character for the number eight means "luck," First Interstate developed a checking account featuring account numbers that begin with 888. The account is available to customers statewide. The new account was introduced at a bank-sponsored Chinese Moon Festival celebration. The Moon Festival, celebrated worldwide on September 20, recalls the stories of many characters associated with the moon in Asian mythology. Modern Chinese celebrate the

Moon Festival as a family reunion, somewhat like a Western Thanksgiving. The event was very popular with Chinese-American customers and their families.

- The bank also developed a new series of 10 Chinese-language brochures, a mortgage especially for immigrants who have not yet obtained permanent legal-resident status, and cash-secured credit cards especially designed for new U.S. residents.

What can you do?   How can you begin to expand your knowledge of various cultural holidays? How can knowing about festivals, holidays, and other events assist you?

Action Steps: _____

_____

ATTRACTIONS

Fiesta Texas
San Antonio, Texas

Fiesta Texas, an entertainment theme park known as "The Town Built Just For Fun," nestled in the Texas Hill Country in a beautiful canyon setting, provides entertainment to the residents of San Antonio, who boast a large Hispanic and German population, as well as to their other Texan and international visitors. Heidi Stipetic, Training Department at Fiesta Texas, says, "We strive to meet the needs of these guests as well as our other international customers. Our quest for service excellence has just begun and our commitment to service quality is strengthening every day. Our vision at Fiesta Texas is to provide WOW service to each and every internal and external guest."

Here's what they are doing:

- The park employs ethnically diverse and multilingual employees, called Cast Members.

8

- Cast Members wear name tags that have the languages they speak printed on them.

- Language lists are kept at Hospitality, Guest Relations, EMS, Loss Prevention Base, Operations Base, and Personnel for easy reference and assignment of Cast Member to guest. Language lists also include a listing of Cast Members who speak sign language.

- The Amigo Program is made up of multilingual Cast Members who assist guests with any problems or concerns and take care of those problems or concerns right on the spot.

- The Park entertainment is representative of the cultural traditions of Texas and includes, for instance, a Lone Star Christmas Show, which explores the Hispanic, German and Old West traditions of San Antonio.

- Foreign currency exchange is available inside the Park.

- A variety of German, Hispanic, and American cuisine is provided throughout the park.

HOTELS AND RESORTS

The Walt Disney World Swan and Dolphin Lake Buena Vista, Florida

At the Walt Disney World Swan and Dolphin, world-class hospitality is both a commitment and a reality. The basic standard of service for every customer is excellence. Part of the service excellence includes special efforts to make multicultural visitors feel at home. As a result of its commitment to make guests more comfortable and to attract more business, the resort has become a favorite destination of Japanese visitors traveling to Florida.

Here's how they do it:

- Resort staff travel extensively and pay attention to the little things. For example, in Japan, a desirable room is a smoking room, furnished with twin beds, and above the lobby level. Amenities include green tea, a Japanese hot pot for making the tea, a Yucata kimono robe and slippers. This type of room and amenities are available for Japanese guests at the Swan and Dolphin, and an in-language newspaper is delivered to the guest's room.

- Employees try to understand the culture of the visitor. By learning about the culture, hotel staff can anticipate special needs and requests and can provide service that is polite and meaningful. For instance, the front desk staff does not require their Japanese guests to provide a credit card to register. To do so would be confusing and insulting as well, indicating that the guest was not honorable or trustworthy.

- As part of an ongoing commitment to multicultural customer service, the resort employs a full-time Japanese cultural specialist who walks through the resort, dines in the restaurants, previews plans for special events, and assists employees and guests with questions and special requests. When she encounters a situation that may have an unanticipated meaning for Japanese guests, she uses it as an opportunity to customize the hotel service and educate the staff. For example, the color theme planned for a Japanese convention event was black and white. Knowing that this color combination is used for funeral occasions in Japan, the cultural specialist helped the convention staff select a more culturally appropriate decor for the event.

- A culture of continuous learning exists at Swan and Dolphin. Efforts include employee newsletter articles on topics such as Japanese holidays, greetings, foods, culture, and key words in the language. Language training is provided for housekeeping, coffee shop, front desk, and other customer contact staff members. Employees also know that they can call on the cultural specialist at any time to learn more about and meet the needs of customers.

- Learning from your customers is the best way to find out what would make their visit more comfortable. However, some customers may not express themselves directly to you. They may choose a more indirect approach such as speaking to their travel agent or

8

tour coordinator about your service. Both forms of customer feed-back can help improve your service delivery.

What can you do?   Anticipating the needs of customers and adapting both delivery style and delivery systems, helps to create world class service. What can you do to anticipate the needs of your guests?

Action Steps:_____

_____

Alexis Hotel
Seattle, Washington

People in all major countries of the world, with the exception of the United States, use the centigrade (Celsius) temperature measurement system. When in the United States or when reading brochures about the United States, our use of the Fahrenheit temperature scale is "foreign" to them. Providing temperature, size, distance, or other measurements to customers in a familiar format is a helpful service.

Each evening, the Alexis Hotel in Seattle provides a weather card for visitors so that they can dress appropriately or plan their day according to weather conditions. By using both Fahrenheit and Celsius measurements, along with visual depictions, all guests benefit from this helpful information.

Here's a sample:

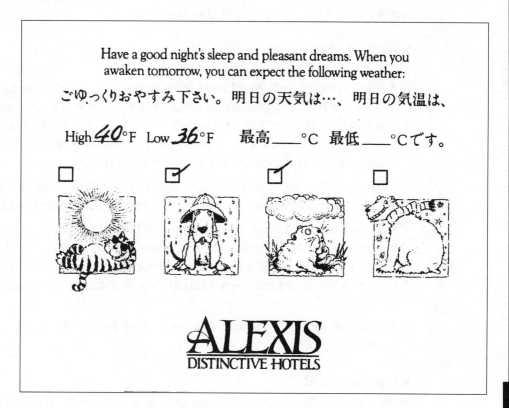

Have a good night's sleep and pleasant dreams. When you
awaken tomorrow, you can expect the following weather:

ごゆっくりおやすみ下さい。 明日の天気は…、 明日の気温は、

High _40_°F Low _36_°F   最高＿＿°C 最低＿＿°Cです。

ALEXIS
DISTINCTIVE HOTELS

8

MUSEUMS

Salvador Dali Museum
St. Petersburg, Florida

Over 45 percent of all visitors to the Dali Museum are international. With
relatively little expense, the museum has positioned itself as a favorite of
international visitors to the region.

In the 1980s, there were very few international visitors to the museum,
even though its content appeared to be of interest to visitors from around
the world. The museum found out that few international visitors to Florida

knew about it. Wayne Atherholt, director of marketing and public relations, knew it was time to get the word out.

Here's what they did:

- They created rack brochures in multiple languages. The print pieces were designed so that only a single plate change was needed to change the brochure's language. This kept production costs low. Translation was provided by several international tour companies in exchange for free museum tickets.

- They invited international students from a nearby tourism school to visit the museum and critique its services and marketing.

- They built long-term relationships with international tour operators, agents, and media. They provided museum tours and training and foreign-language materials to tour operators and translated brochures, press releases, and articles to foreign travel agents and travel media.

- They recruited museum volunteers from the multicultural community.

What can you do?

What can you do to get the word out about your product or service to multicultural and international customers? Who else in the community can you work with to attract and serve multicultural customers? What can you do to make visitors feel more welcome?

Action Steps:_____

_____

8

Chapter 8 Checkpoints

✓ Many service providers have already adapted their service delivery style or method to provide quality service to all of their customers.

✓ Many organizations have created and implemented a variety of policies, procedures, and practices that assist their customer service representatives in meeting the needs of their multicultural customers, patients, and guests.

✓ You can begin now to incorporate many of these ideas into the way you provide quality service to all of your customers.

✓ You can continually share and learn new ideas and methods from others that allow you to expand your thinking and adapt your style to meet the needs of a continually growing and changing customer base.

A | Comments about Scenarios

CHAPTER 1

Tanisha, Cashier in a Department Store (page 1)

Customers have varying expectations concerning the degree of service they need or will receive. What is good customer service to one customer may not be to another. It can never be assumed that one size fits all when working with people. All customers appreciate meaningful, sincere answers to their questions. In this situation, the customer appeared both surprised and pleased that Tanisha knew the products and could be helpful even though she was not in the clothing department. Tanisha showed flexibility and a sincere willingness to be helpful.

CHAPTER 2

Robert, Receptionist in a Doctor's Office (page 13)

Using customers' names may represent a significant moment of truth for them. Robert was following what he thought to be friendly customer service techniques. Robert himself may enjoy being called by his first name, but many multicultural customers prefer the use of last names until permission is given or a relationship is established that invites less formality. Many times last names are avoided because of difficulty in pronouncing them. Introducing yourself and asking for assistance in pronouncing unfamiliar names, even if your pronunciation is somewhat rough, will show the customer that you care enough to try and that you respect individual wishes.

CHAPTER 3

Regina, Hotel Front Desk Clerk (page 23)

In Japan, desirable rooms are generally located above the lobby level while less desirable rooms are situated on lower floors. Regina was not aware that her customers perceived that a part of the delegation had been assigned to lower-class rooms. Also, Regina did not realize that the customers did not confront her directly because they felt a more respectful and appropriate way to communicate their dissatisfaction was through an intermediary, the group coordinator. When asked to upgrade their rooms, Regina made the assumption (based on her own experience) that there was no reason to move the guests. Had she stopped to consider that there may be additional cultural considerations, she could have explored different room options with her guests. Understanding Japanese customs and communication style would help Regina anticipate and meet the needs of these and future customers.

Craig, Trade Show Representative (page 34)

Craig's stereotype is that all Asians are the same or that all Asians speak Japanese. Of course, what we often refer to as Asia is a huge region covering 16 million square miles with over 2 billion inhabitants. Asia includes Japan, the People's Republic of China, North and South Korea, Vietnam, Taiwan, Indonesia, the Philippines, Malaysia, India, Singapore, Hong Kong, and other Pacific Basin countries. The diversity of the people is immense, both between countries and within countries. Many different languages are spoken. As a result of Craig's stereotyping, there is a good chance that he insulted some of his potential customers from areas of Asia other than Japan. At the least, he appeared naive and inexperienced. Craig should (1) try to recognize his stereotypes and how they affect his behavior, (2) continue learning about Asia, (3) use his knowledge of culture as a guideline only, and (4) take time to find out where his customers or potential customers are from.

Joanne, Jewelry Store Sales Representative
(page 35)

Stereotypes are not limited to international customers. Several stereotypes could explain why Joanne offered different payment options to the white male and the black female. Joanne may believe that white customers or male customers have the cash or credit history to make purchases while African-American or female customers do not. While Joanne may not be aware of the difference in the way she treated the two customers, customers do notice. Women and ethnic minority customers commonly report demeaning stereotypical treatment in stores, banks, sports clubs, doctors' offices, car dealerships, and restaurants, just to name a few places.

Tomica, Bank New Accounts Representative
(page 35)

Tomica's stereotypes are age based. She feels that all young people will not be interested in certain bank services. As a result, she withholds information from her younger customers that she makes available to older customers. Because of this belief, the younger customer is given fewer choices and does not learn about services he may wish to utilize now or later. Both Tomica and her organization miss out on the opportunity to promote and sell additional bank services. This has a direct impact on customer relations and on the organization's bottom line.

CHAPTER 4

Kathy, Customer Relations Planner (page 39)

At first glance, the menu looks delicious to Kathy. As she looks more closely, however, she realizes that several customer groups will not be able to enjoy the banquet. Each course includes pork products or shellfish, which are unacceptable for many Jewish, Seventh-Day Adventists, or Muslim clients. The menu offers few or no choices for cultural or religious groups or individuals who are vegetarian. Also, individuals on low-fat diets will find few low-fat alternatives. Since the purpose of this event is to build client goodwill, Kathy should select a menu that will be acceptable to a large range of clients. She has already taken the most important step by raising the question, "How will my decision affect *all* of my customers—those who are like me and those who are not?"

Susan, Information Counter Representataive (page 42)

Susan has just delivered very poor service. She interrupted the customer, she passed him off to someone else, she assumed he *did not* speak English well, she assumed he *did* speak Spanish, and she did not ask him whether he would like language assistance. The customer may be embarrassed by Susan's judgment of his English. Possibly he's insulted by her apparent unwillingness to assist him. The customer service barrier here is Susan's lack of knowledge and skill in serving multicultural customers. In the future, Susan can provide the same level of attention and assistance to customers with accents as she gives to other customers. If there are true language difficulties, she can ask the customer if she would like language assistance, find out the customer's language, and then seek Maria's assistance, if indeed the customer speaks Spanish.

Rob, Department Store Sales Representative (page 42)

In this store, the check-cashing policy is a barrier to providing outstanding multicultural customer service. The policy negatively affects international tourists and businesspeople who do not have U.S. licenses. Elderly shoppers who no longer drive, some customers with disabilities who do not drive, and visitors who utilize mass transit instead of driving may also be excluded. These customers are likely to feel inconvenienced and possibly not appreciated; some may feel annoyed enough to take their business elsewhere. Rob should try to be diplomatic when explaining this policy to customers. He should bring this item to management's attention along with suggestions for change. Possible acceptable forms of ID include a passport, employment ID, voter registration card, Social Security card, and other municipal or federal documents.

Tina, Restaurant Seating Hostess (page 43)

Several barriers prevent Tina from providing outstanding customer service to this family. First, the product itself—the food—is not flexible enough to meet the needs of this family. Second, Tina lacks the knowledge to be able to recommend another restaurant. And possibly, Tina's restaurant training did not prepare her sufficiently to deal with customers who have special requests. Tina and her management should recognize the impact of the lost business, adapt their menu to include additional items, or allow the chef to respond to special customer requests. They could also learn about nearby restaurants that accommodate special dietary needs.

CHAPTER 5

Carla, Rental Car Agency Customer Service Representative (page 53)

Carla's international customers have different expectations and needs than her other customers. Carla should realize that cars vary from country to country and that international visitors may be unfamiliar with the American cars and car rental procedures. Carla will need to learn to anticipate their needs and to adapt her service delivery to better meet her customers' needs. Carla can utilize the four-step process for identifying and meeting multicultural customer needs that is explained later in Chapter 5.

CHAPTER 6

Thomas, Bellman at Vacation Ownership Resort (page 71)

By American cultural rules, Thomas' behavior represents friendly, helpful customer service. However, he made several gestures and nonverbal signals that are highly impolite in Middle Eastern culture. Thus, he insulted his customers without even knowing it. For example, signaling with the finger is very degrading. He used his left hand to take the car keys and the luggage, to give the parking ticket to the father, and to signal the family. In many parts of the Middle East, the left hand is reserved for personal hygiene and is not used to take or give items or to touch or signal others. Finally, Thomas' manners were so relaxed and friendly, including toward the female members of the party, that he appeared to be insolent and overstepping his bounds.

Hotel Front Desk (page 72)

Communication styles vary across cultures. Most Americans feel fairly comfortable verbalizing a complaint; they feel it is the first step toward resolving a problem. In many Asian cultures, making a complaint about the way someone is treating you would be impolite and inappropriate, causing embarrassment for all concerned. Due to the importance of harmony in the Japanese culture, these customers would prefer not to cause embarrassment, even if it means being inconvenienced. However, there is a very good chance these customers will not return to this hotel and will inform other Japanese customers of their experience. In the tightly knit Japanese communities, this negative word of mouth will be even more damaging than in the American marketplace.

CHAPTER SEVEN

Gerald, Customer Service Representative
(page 87)

Gerald has made the same mistakes that many customer service providers make when helping customers who do not speak English as their first language. First, he speaks louder in an attempt to help the customer understand. Second, he immediately calls in a bilingual co-worker to help this customer before he knows the customer's language or language needs. Although Gerald's intent is good, the impact on the customer is not. In the future, Gerald can adapt the way he speaks and the way he listens to better serve foreign-language customers. If language difficulties are insurmountable or if the customer would like interpretation, Gerald can utilize interpretation. However, he should avoid assuming that every customer with an accent needs or wants language assistance.

B | More Multicultural Resources

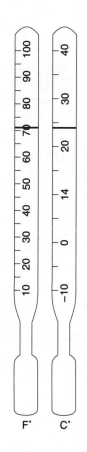

F° C°

TEMPERATURE

How to convert Fahrenheit to centigrade

Formula: (Temperature in F° − 32) × 5/9

_____ − 32 = _____ × 5/9 = _____

Sample: 85° Fahrenheit equals 29.4 degrees centigrade

Step 1:   85 − 32 = 53

Step 2:   53 × 5/9 = 29.44

How to convert centigrade to Fahrenheit

Formula: (Temperature in C° + 32) × 9/5

_____ + 32 = _____ × 9/5

Sample: 23° centigrade equals 70.7 degrees Fahrenheit

Step 1:   23 + 32 = 55

Step 2:   55 × 9/5 = 70.71

Often, you can look at a thermometer that shows both Fahrenheit and Centigrade.

INTERNATIONAL CLOTHING SIZE EQUIVALENTS

Men

Men's Suits and Overcoats

American	36	38	40	42	44	46
British	36	38	40	42	44	46
Continental	46	48	50	52	54	56

Men's Socks

American	9½	10	10½	11	11½
British	9½	10	10½	11	11½
Continental	38–39	39–40	40–41	41–42	42–43

Men's Shoes

American	8	8½	9	9½	10	10½	11	11½	12
British	7	7½		8½		9½		10½	11
Continental	41	42		43		44		45	46

Women

Women's Suits and Dresses

American	4	6	8	10	12	14	16	18
British			10	12	14	16	18	20
Continental			38	40	42	44	46	48

Women's Hosiery

American	8	8½	9	9½	10	10½
British	8	8½	9	9½	10	10½
Continental	0	1	2	3	4	5

Women's Shoes

American	6	6½	7	7½	8	8½	9	9½	10
British	4½	5	5½	6	6½	7			
Continental	38	38	39	39	40	41			

Children

American	4	6	8	10	12	14
British						
Height (inches)	43	48	55	58	60	62
Age	4–5	6–7	9–10	11	12	13
Continental						
Height (cm)	125	135	150	155	160	165
Age	7	9	12	13	14	15

INTERNATIONAL CALLS

International business people and tourists traveling in the United States may ask you to help them place an international call from the United States. Or you may need to contact one of your international clients in her own country. Here are instructions for placing direct-dial international calls:

Digit to get an outside line, if required	011 for an international call	country code (1 to 4 digits)	city code (1 to 5 digits)	telephone number

There are a few things to keep in mind when dialing internationally:

- Often the city code starts with a 0, which is dropped when the call is placed from the United States. For example, although the country code for Japan is listed on business cards as 081, it becomes 81 when dialed from the United States. (There are a few exceptions to the "drop the zero" rule, such as Moscow city code 095.)

- Many people are confused by telephone numbers around the world. Although the United States always has seven-digit phone numbers, telephone numbers around the world range from three to eight numbers.
- For international country codes, refer to a country code chart or call your long-distance telephone operator.

DIRECT-DIAL COUNTRY CODE

Andorra	33	Ajman / Fujairah / Sharjah / Umm-Al-Quwain	971	Argentina	54	Australia	61
Austria	43	Bahrain	973	Belgium	32	Belize	501
Brazil	55	Chile	56	China, Rep. of	86	Colombia	57
Costa Rica	506	Cuba	53	Cyprus	357	Denmark	45
Dubai	978	Ecuador	593	El Salvador	503	Fiji Islands	679
Finland	358	France	33	Germany	49	Greece	30
Guam	671	Guatemala	502	Haiti	509	Honduras	504
Hong Kong	852	Iran	98	Iraq	964	Ireland	353
Israel	972	Italy	39	Japan	81	Kenya	254
Korea	82 / 850	Kuwait	965	Liechtenstein	41	Luxembourg	352
Malaysia	60	Monaco	33	Netherlands	31	Netherlands Antilles	599
New Zealand	64	Nicaragua	505	Norway	47	Papua New Guinea	675
Peru	51	Philippines	63	Portugal	351	Russia	7
San Marino	39	Saudi Arabia	966	Singapore	65	South Africa	27
Spain	34	Sweden	46	Switzerland	41	Tahiti	689
Thailand	66	Turkey	90	United Arab Emirates / Abu Dhabi	971	United Kingdom	44
Vatican City	39	Venezuela	58				

World Time Zone Map

Use this map for easy identification of world time zones. It can help you determine the local time where you are calling. Remember to subtract one hour for every time zone you cross going westward (right to left). Conversely, you must add one hour for every time zone you cross going eastward (left to right). For example, if you are calling from New York City at 9AM, it is 2 PM in London, and 10 PM in Hong Kong.

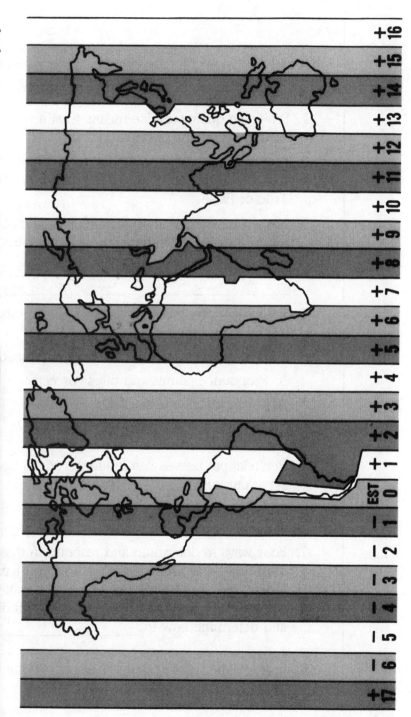

Post-Test

Complete the following to assess your understanding of the knowledge and skills required to serve multicultural customers.

1. Providing quality service means treating all customers the same so that everything is standardized.   True or False

2. Multicultural customer service means understanding that a customer's needs and expectations may vary across cultures.
True or False

3. Name four ways that your multicultural customers' needs may differ from the customers you may have traditionally served.

   _____, _____,
   _____, _____.

4. Four easy ways to begin to serve your multicultural customers are to:

   a. Find out their preferred way of being addressed and use it.

   b. Pronounce names and titles correctly.

   c. Err on the side of formality.

   d. _____ .

5. Personal pet peeves can influence our behavior and the way we serve our customers.   True or False

6. We are born with behaviors and attitudes that are consistent with our culture.   True or False

7. Four ways to determine and respond to the needs of multicultural customers are to describe how you typically help a customer, identify assumptions you might make, check your assumptions to see if they are true for the individual customer, and determine how to _____
_____ .

8. In the United States alone, there are 70 languages spoken.
True or False

9. When working with customers who do not speak English as their first language, you can adapt your own manner of speaking and _____.

10. Most people use nonverbal communication as the universal language that is understood the same by everyone.
True or False

ANSWER TO POST-TEST

1. False.   2. True.
3. Differences in language, protocol and courtesy, religion, communication style (verbal/nonverbal), logistical needs (currency, transportation, measurement systems, and sizing), culture (food, holiday, rituals, and celebrations), others.
4. Avoid assuming.   5. True.
6. False. (Culture is learned.)
7. Adapt your customer service to meet each customer's needs.
8. False. More than 140 languages are spoken.
9. Listening.   10. False.

Bibliography

Albrecht, Karl. *Service Within*. Homewood, IL: Business One Irwin, 1990.

Albrecht, Karl. *The Only Thing That Matters: Bringing the Power of the Customer into the Center of Your Business*. New York: Harper Business, 1992.

Albrecht, Karl, and Ron Zemke. *Service America! Doing Business in the New Economy*. Homewood, IL: Dow Jones-Irwin, 1985.

Axtell, Roger. E. *Do's and Taboos around the World*. New York: John Wiley & Sons, 1990.

Brislan, Richard W., and Tomoko Yoshida (editors). *Improving Intercultural Interaction: Modules for Cross-Cultural Training Programs*. Thousand Oaks, CA: Sage, 1994.

Bryson, Bill. *The Mother Tongue: English and How It Got That Way*. New York: William Morrow, 1990.

Chan-Herur, K.C. *Communicating with Customers around the World*. San Francisco: AuMonde International Publishing, 1994.

Gardenswartz, Lee, and Anita Rowe. *Managing Diversity: A Complete Desk Reference and Planning Guide*. (Homewood, IL: Business One Irwin New York/San Diego/Pfeiffer & Company, 1993).

The Multicultural Customer (video). Santa Monica, CA: Salenger Films, 1993.

Multicultural Resource Book & Appointment Calendar. Amherst, MA: Amherst Educational Publishing, 1994 (published annually).

Renwick, George W. (editor), *Interacts* (series). Yarmouth, ME: Intercultural Press, 1984–1994. Series includes the following titles:
Spain Is Different
Encountering the Chinese: A Guide for Americans
Understanding Arabs: A Guide for Westerners
Considering Filipinos
From Nyet to Da: Understanding the Russians
From Da to Yes: Understanding the East Europeans.
A Common Core: Thais and Americans
Border Crossings: American Interactions with Israelis
Good Neighbors: Communicating with the Mexicans
With Respect to the Japanese: A Guide for Americans
A Fair Go for All: Australian and American Interactions.

Rossman, Marlene L. *Multicultural Marketing: Selling to a Diverse America*. New York: American Management Association, 1994.

Sewell, Carl. *Customers for Life*. New York: Pocket Books, 1990.

Simons, George. *Working Together: How to Become More Effective in a Multicultural Organization*. Los Altos, CA: Crisp, 1989.

Simons, George; Carmen Vazquez; and Philip Harris. *Transcultural Leadership: Empowering the Diverse Workforce*. Houston: Gulf Publishing, 1993.

Statistical Abstact of the U.S. (114th edition). Washington, DC: U.S. Department of Commerce, 1994.

Thiederman, Sondra. *Bridging Cultural Barriers for Corporate Success: How to Manage the Multicultural Work Force*. New York: Lexington Books, 1991.

Thiederman, Sondra. *Profiting in America's Multicultural Marketplace: How to Do Business across Cultural Lines*. New York: Lexington Books, 1991.

World of Gestures (video). Berkeley: University of California Extension Center for Media and Independent Learning, 1991.

Zemke, Ron, and Chip R. Bell. *Service Wisdom*. Minneapolis: Lakewood Publications, 1990.

Business Skills Express Series

This growing series of books addresses a broad range of key business skills and topics to meet the needs of employees, human resource departments, and training consultants.

To obtain information about these and other Business Skills Express books, please call Irwin Professional Publishing toll free at 1-800-634-3966.

Effective Performance Management
ISBN 1-55623-867-3

Hiring the Best
ISBN 1-55623-865-7

Writing that Works
ISBN 1-55623-856-8

Customer Service Excellence
ISBN 1-55623-969-6

Writing for Business Results
ISBN 1-55623-854-1

Powerful Presentation Skills
ISBN 1-55623-870-3

Meetings that Work
ISBN 1-55623-866-5

Effective Teamwork
ISBN 1-55623-880-0

Time Management
ISBN 1-55623-888-6

Assertiveness Skills
ISBN 1-55623-857-6

Motivation at Work
ISBN 1-55623-868-1

Overcoming Anxiety at Work
ISBN 1-55623-869-X

Positive Politics at Work
ISBN 1-55623-879-7

Telephone Skills at Work
ISBN 1-55623-858-4

Managing Conflict at Work
ISBN 1-55623-890-8

The New Supervisor: Skills for Success
ISBN 1-55623-762-6

The *Americans with Disabilities Act*: What Supervisors Need to Know
ISBN 1-55623-889-4

Managing the Demands of Work and Home
ISBN 0-7863-0221-6

Effective Listening Skills
ISBN 0-7863-0102-4

Goal Management at Work
ISBN 0-7863-0225-9

Positive Attitudes at Work
ISBN 0-7863-0100-8

Supervising the Difficult Employee
ISBN 0-7863-0219-4

Cultural Diversity in the Workplace
ISBN 0-7863-0125-2

Managing Change in the Workplace
ISBN 0-7863-0162-7

Negotiating for Business Results
ISBN 0-7863-0114-7

Practical Business Communication

ISBN 0-7863-0227-5

High Performance Speaking
ISBN 0-7863-0222-4

Delegation Skills
ISBN 0-7863-0105-9

Coaching Skills: A Guide for Supervisors
ISBN 0-7863-0220-8

Customer Service and the Telephone
ISBN 0-7863-0224-0

Creativity at Work
ISBN 0-7863-0223-2

Effective Interpersonal Relationships
ISBN 0-7863-0255-0

The Participative Leader
ISBN 0-7863-0252-6

Building Customer Loyalty
ISBN 0-7863-0253-4

Getting and Staying Organized
ISBN 0-7863-0254-2

Business Etiquette
ISBN 0-7863-0323-9

Empowering Employees
ISBN 0-7863-0314-X

Training Skills for Supervisors
ISBN 0-7863-0313-1

Moving Meetings
ISBN 0-7863-0333-6

Multicultural Customer Service
ISBN 0-7863-0332-8